Build the Brain
the Common Core Way

Build the Brain
the Common Core Way

Pamela Nevills

CORWIN
A SAGE Company

CORWIN
A SAGE Company

FOR INFORMATION:

Corwin
A SAGE Company
2455 Teller Road
Thousand Oaks, California 91320
(800) 233-9936
www.corwin.com

SAGE Publications Ltd.
1 Oliver's Yard
55 City Road
London EC1Y 1SP
United Kingdom

SAGE Publications India Pvt. Ltd.
B 1/I 1 Mohan Cooperative Industrial Area
Mathura Road, New Delhi 110 044
India

SAGE Publications Asia-Pacific Pte. Ltd.
3 Church Street
#10-04 Samsung Hub
Singapore 049483

Printed in the United States of America

A catalog record of this book is available from the Library of Congress.

ISBN 978-1-4833-5296-1

This book is printed on acid-free paper.

Acquisitions Editor: Jessica Allan
Associate Editor: Kimberly Greenberg
Editorial Assistant: Cesar Reyes
Production Editor: Amy Schroller
Copy Editor: Deanna Noga
Typesetter: C&M Digitals (P) Ltd.
Proofreader: Rae Ann Goodwin
Indexer: Rick Hurd
Cover Designer: Shawn Girsberger

SFI Certified Sourcing
www.sfiprogram.org
SFI-00453

14 15 16 17 18 10 9 8 7 6 5 4 3 2 1

Contents

Foreword

What a historic time for education in the USA! The Common Core State Standards, new assessments to measure how well students are learning them, and neuroscience is edging out behavioral psychology as a major driver of pedagogy. As educators search for some help through such major transitions, Pamela Nevills's new book offers great understanding and insight to guide educators to success in increasing student learning in the 21st century. Pamela's previous work linking brain research to improve the teaching of reading has helped an endless number of teachers gain discernment in instructional practice for literacy. Her successful application of applying some basic brain anatomical functions, and memory models, combined with her experience and research of best practices, brought a new and valuable perspective to teaching students how to read at various grade levels. Being ahead of her time, it's obvious that she is excited now that such perspectives are being applied to the Common Core Standards and "the art of teaching can be unleashed as teachers call on their own thinking brains."

This book will help prepare teachers for the new demands on students' brains as they take on standards that elevate thinking and problem solving above rote memorization. I am particularly impressed with how Pamela is able to pinpoint the key instructional shift that the Common Core Standards demand: students talking more to respond to increasing depths of knowledge and inquiry. I look forward to the great realization that English learners talking much more in class about their learning will wonderfully impact their English fluency. Brain research has long touted the value of writing, and now the Common Core is emphasizing it, too. Nevills also connects this to how learning spaces will need to adapt to support all this deeper learning. Instead of applying the findings from neuroscience to just reading, Pamela Nevills's work here can be applied across the curriculum.

Also, *Build the Brain the Common Core Way* is not just about applying an understanding of the brain to teaching students. A critical part of implementing the new standards is applying this understanding to professional development for educators. I use the term *educators* rather than teachers because I believe this book can help administrators as well as those in higher education who are responsible for preparing teachers. In fact, I look forward to a time soon when basic understanding of how the brain learns will be common knowledge among parents.

We are experiencing a major shift in education in the United States, and much of it is driven by an increased awareness of how the brain learns. Again and again I have witnessed the application of such awareness to school systems result in continuous improvement of student learning. This book will provide a comforting understanding of why the Common Core will be successful; it will require students to think. How the brain learns and thinks is the basis for our district's curriculum, instructional and assessment decisions, and is the foundation for our continued success.

Now, Pamela Nevills's work can help you implement the Common Core Standards and improve learning and skills your students will need to succeed in the 21st century.

—Justin Cunningham, EdD

Justin Cunningham, EdD, Superintendent,
Bonsall Unified School District

Small School Districts' Association Outstanding
Superintendent of the Year, 2013

Preface

It is uncommon to find books by teachers for teachers. Expert teachers are doing all they can do to keep up with their teaching. When they pass a group of students to the next level they enter a phase of regeneration for the new group in the fall. Many books about teaching are by nonclassroom authors: retired teachers, consultants, researchers, psychologists, district personnel, or university professors. To read, gather resources, review or conduct research, access experience, investigate, validate, and turn a mountain of information into something meaningful and readable for teachers and people in charge of educational systems takes more than tenacity; it takes boatloads of thoughtful, reflective TIME.

There is an innate excitement, passion for learning, and yearning to get to work that exists in learners who are engaged with a significant project. Students who are fortunate enough to be in school programs that ignite them with desire to know and discover feel this way. I felt just like that about this project, writing this book. It started as I read and heard more and more about the Common Core State Standards (CCSS). My interest piqued as I realized that this is a significant change—a conglomerate of individuals have taken ahold of revamping educational priorities and deemed that children need to learn at substantially higher levels of thinking. I wanted to know how this happened. Chapter 3 is the result of my research into what the common core is, and what it is not. Also, the movers and shakers were identified: foundations, state governors, universities, and educational agencies; all working together to say, "Enough!" Students simply are not prepared for the constantly changing world that exists for them as adults or as college or career learners.

UNIFY EDUCATIONAL PRACTICE WITH BRAIN SCIENCE

My excitement intensified as I grabbed ahold of the implications for my professional career passion, unifying educational practice with information from neuroscience. If students need to develop deep thinking skills, become critical thinkers, and be able to validate and talk about their thinking, then the neuroscience of learning is painstakingly relevant and necessary. There are "neurosceptics" who would like education to wait and not apply brain research to the classroom until we have better understanding of how the human brain learns (Dayal, 2013). There is no validity to their concerns. Although some have misinterpreted brain science research and caused the public to be swayed by "neuromyths," there is enough purposeful information for neuroscientists and educators to unite, converse, and share professional evidence. The new field of neuroeducation has been birthed.

If education held to this "let's wait" interpretation, there would be no common core. The CCSS are based on a premise that there are answers and there are more answers, and there are correct answers that have not yet been discovered. Knowing that does not hold learners from learning foundational elements for each of education's subjects. Such are the "big questions" that teachers are encouraged by the common core to pose to their students. Some simple answers are correct, but not complete. As students progress through their education years they revisit the questions that are not yet solved adequately, and grapple with them once again for more in-depth answers. Neuroscientists will continue to expand on what they currently know about how the human brain learns, and educators can gain more insight into the mysteries of the mind. But let's enjoy what we now know and put it to use.

There are many well established truths from neuroscience that help teachers be better directors of learning. Teachers can understand working and long-term memory. They can use information about neuroplasticity to inform their classroom practices. Knowing that active engagement stimulates neuron networks in specified places in the human brain encourages them to plan activities that request students to be active in their learning. Understanding why some students are attentive and are able to filter unneeded distractive sensory input and that other students have trouble staying on task is useful information. Helping students know how to help themselves develop as competent learners is important work that makes sense when it is put in "brain terms." All these insights came together in Chapter 4. With this on paper, I eagerly continued to write about all that was bubbling inside my head.

EARLY ADOPTERS FOR THE COMMON CORE

Next, I needed to know what was happening already across the nation. My digging and investigative efforts yielded great rewards. There are some early implementers who are bold in their teaching and/or learning approaches. And they care enough to share their efforts. My daughter, who teaches high school courses, teacher friends, and colleagues validated what I learned as I visited professional conversations at social networking sites. All this information is so available, so inviting, and so important for what is happening across the nation with this educational reform movement. Realize that the common core has the most potential to make a difference for students that I have experienced in all my years of education. And, unlike previous books I authored, most of my resources have a website attached to them. This is a dangerous spot to be in, because they all have to be verified at the time of printing, and I hope they remain available to the reader. Learning and producing are so different in the age of computers and electronics. The common core begs for classroom projects that take advantage of all that is there for the students.

COMMON CORE RESOURCE

This book is a resource for every teacher. It is intended to spark their energy for the entire common core implementation process by empowering them and exciting them about their role, their potential. Principals and other administrators are encouraged to see the talent and persistence in their teachers. Readers will find enticing, fresh teaching strategies particularly in Chapters 4, 5, and 6. These ideas beg to be tried immediately, because they are easy to implement and powerful for student learners. Teachers need to thirst for more ways they can provide interesting, quality experiences for their learners as they are expressed in the common core expectations. They have more reason to collaborate. Professional relationships will thrive as the curriculum is completed and an instructional scope and sequence emerges that has not been provided through the common core. A new way of doing school, by shifting the focus from how teachers perform as lesson presenters to how students behave, as the actor/learners on center stage is an extreme change.

Chapter 1 draws the reader's interest with something different, changes in perception for how we do school. It invites school personnel to challenge their thinking from what we have always done to the potential of the common core. A further look at common core expectations leads to what teachers will need to do to retool in Chapter 2. In this chapter, teachers are challenged to plan their lessons differently, and for those who evaluate teachers to turn their focus on what students are doing to learn. Each chapter has strategies and activities that can be used immediately. After a thorough look at the common core in Chapter 3, the reader learns or revisits some of what neurology has to offer education. Neuroscientists have provided abundant insights from what they have discovered about the act of learning. Knowing what is going on when students engage in active thinking gives teachers an advantage in planning and directing classroom activities. This is the intent of Chapter 4, How Learning Happens.

The next chapter was a lot of fun to write, because it accepts the premise of "learning is all about what is happening for students." It provides a new way to design lesson or big unit study that fits the common core requirements. It is filled with practical, try-this-now ideas. Chapter 5 talks about what teachers can do. It is followed by what the students can do in Chapter 6. This one has a somewhat whimsical excitement with even more gratifying possibilities than the previous one. But do not be misled; there are serious activities for students with respect for the important learning that must be done. Readers are challenged as directors of learning to place their students in situations that draw them into intense involvement as learners.

The following chapter, Powerful Staff Development for Adult Learners, is intriguing because it looks specifically at professional teachers as learners. Teachers are promoted to be leaders of their peers during workshops and supported by research and best practice to do so. Chapter 8 talks about the very change process itself and how school districts can articulate vision and direction while providing support services. A soft change is described as school personnel move incrementally to meet the CCSS expectations. The system directing common core implementation is challenged to move steadily, purposefully, and incrementally over time.

This book is a resource for every educator and encourages them to jump start the entire common core process. It plants a desire for teachers to take a fresh look at learning and promotes confidence by identifying all the skills teachers already possess. The American Educator (2013) addressed teachers' perceptions of the common core. Members of American Federation of Teachers (AFT) responded to a survey about the CCSS and overwhelmingly supported it. While 78% of the teachers said they already received staff development related to the CCSS, less than half, 43%, felt the training was adequate for them to teach to the new standards.

Approaching the common core from a new prospective and comfort level is needed. It is important to listen to friends who are teachers and those exiting the field. I was curious enough to listen in on conversations among teachers through professional Internet exchanges. District websites also provided information about what is available to support the common core. The time is right to gather information and to respond with support. My years as a teacher, staff developer, administrator, and university faculty have allowed me to talk with teachers and be in classrooms nationwide. This is the time to make known what the education system has allowed me to learn through many years of service.

Special Chapter for Brainiacs

I cannot forget Chapter 9, which was developed for the brainiacs and their inquisitive nature. While many readers do not want to be bogged down with some of the intricacies of how the brain functions, there are others who long for more detail. Chapter 9 is the chapter for descriptions and definitions, answers to brain questions, and some current findings that have classroom implications. The inquisitive reader is sent to Chapter 9 in prior chapters, when the details are unnecessary for the purpose of this book but are too interesting to leave out. This information is plucked out and made available in the chapter that culminates this book.

It is a match! Common core expectations and understanding neurology make sense. This is the time for brain science to really impact what is happening in the classroom. Teachers are admonished to make good decisions for the time and energy spent by their students. There is precious little time during the school day to prepare our nation's children capably for the world. If teachers understand what happens when children learn at any grade level and at any level of intensity, teaching practices will improve. It is a powerful time to be a teacher, and a pivotal time to be the recipient of a world-class education through the common core.

Note: Chapter-by-chapter questions for book study groups are available at pamelanevills.com.

About the Author

 **Pamela Nevills** is first and foremost a teacher, working with multiage learners—primary grades through postgraduate and doctoral students. In addition to speaking, writing, and consulting she is on faculty at Brandman University working with students in the doctoral program. She has participated on and has been honored by local and state advisory committees. As a two-time panel member for reading textbook selection for the State of California, she is well versed with state and national content standards. She is a national and international speaker and consultant on topics that include the common core state standards, brain development from birth through adulthood, the brain and reading, school designs for all students, and adult learners. Writing is a recent addition to Nevills's work. She is published with the State of California, the *Journal of Staff Development*, and organizational newsletters, in addition to her work with Corwin. More about her work, chapter-by-chapter study questions for this book and contact information can be found at pamelanevills.com.

Teaching Can Be Like This

1

Teaching is one of the most challenging, yet potentially rewarding of all professions. With the implementation of the Common Core State Standards the very system of education has an exciting opportunity to be free of cumbersome practices, such as "teaching to the test." Teachers are challenged to think differently about learners and to design classrooms that honor the art of teaching and the science of learning. Every teacher and every student is worthy of a school system that is designed to care for and support deep learning and honor the needs of students, while they experience the expansive development of the human brain.

There are exciting things happening in education around the world right now. Education is and always has been something that everyone values and wants for themselves and their children. And almost everyone has an opinion of how the education system can best serve the people. At this particular time new terminology and new visions are emerging as the Common Core State Standards (CCSS) continues to make its debut. Once again there is a stir of excitement and some trepidation. To squelch all the jitters about this current thrust, it is time to look at some of the really great things that are happening in schools. Once the pieces of good classroom practice fall into place the common core fits right into how school works best.

Different Expectations

This is day three of a new study unit. Henry rushes down the corridor, hoping that none of the students have entered the classroom before him. He wants to be there before class begins to review his plan while the students are still mingling or playing outside. It is important that all the materials are laid out and accessible. He hastily reviews the questions he will ask. He analyzes how much time will be needed and if the plan for this lesson will fit into the time allowed. There are just a few precious minutes before the bell rings and everyone will pile into the classroom. This young teacher reflects about the content that was presented during the last class period. He decides how the new information will be provided and plans for a teacher-prepared talk that can be accessed by all the learning teams at 10:15.

As young and inexperienced as he is, he is aware that group interaction is critical as well as there must be time to practice. He is responsible along with the others that everyone in the group understands all content well enough to give it to another classmate in his or her own words. He reviews the plan one last time. When everyone in the group is ready, Henry, as the group leader for this week, knows to ask their teacher to come and review their work. He knows the final activity is for the group to report back to the whole class. Reporting back is scheduled to happen 20 minutes before the class period ends. His group has a mere five minutes to summarize how they worked together and what they learned. He sighs and breaks into a smile as the bell sounds and the doors to the classroom burst open.

This classroom scenario brings anticipation and excitement in a systematic, planned way.

- What is different in the way learning is structured in this classroom?
- What is expected of the students in this classroom?
- What grade level could be assigned for this scenario?
- What level of mastery on a scale of 1 (some) to 5 (quite a bit) could be expected from this kind of student responsibility? How did you determine this score?

Classrooms like this one are replicated when students are given the responsibility to own their own learning without minimizing the very important role of teachers. The professionals are all over this type of learning, but they do not occupy center stage.

REAL SCHOOL EXAMPLES

A perception change is needed as professionals in the field of education place their focus on real learning, deep and extensive learning. This change can happen when the emphasis for schools is changed from what the teacher needs to do to present a lesson to what students are doing to develop deep understanding. A new breed of schools is featured at the popular Edutopia website (edutopia.org). One such example is Mount Desert Elementary School in Northeast Harbor, Maine. This school has consistently outperformed other schools in the state. The school leaders attribute their success to a focus on Social Emotional Learning (SEL). Students' motivation comes from responsive classroom techniques, such as morning meetings, rules and expectations set by the students, focused positive talk, community-based activities, and various classroom choices for students.

At this school learning has been tailored to the needs of every student. This sustainable practice of focusing on social emotional needs has been in place for over 6 years. It is more than just a good idea; it is a way of doing school. A change has been instituted from focusing on how teachers teach to what students do to learn, and it is key to the success of this program.

Why Social Emotional Learning?

A bit of brain knowledge helps respond to this question. Children's, and adults' brains as well, have an emotional area that is primary to how they feel and react in any situation. Unless this area, the amygdala, is neutralized, it can override other parts of the brain, even the frontal areas where executive thinking and ultimately deep learning occurs. When a child feels safe, somewhat in control of the environment, and feels valued, then the primary needs of the social brain are satisfied. Reaching this plateau allows children to be open to the activities in the classroom. Learning has a robust potential to occur (see Chapter 9, Social Emotional Learning). When children are given the opportunity to contribute to essential activities in the classroom, such as setting the rules and expectations, being asked to define different ways of moving around the elementary classroom, selecting a learning activity for the unit of study in middle school, for example, they feel important and valued. When someone greets them with a sincere concern for their well-being, they are more likely to relax and be open to learning. Customizing the school day to allow students to pursue their own interests is a common strategy in districts that have received award grants from the federal government in the Race to the Top project. Learn more about activities that result from this government project in Chapter 3.

Now teachers have an opportunity to break from rigid lists and step-by-step teaching to experience how they can be true facilitators of deep student learning. The common core advances education to bring out the innovative, creative teaching side of the profession and to apply it to what students need for deep understanding and learning. The educational experience is extended by encouraging inner connectivity among school subjects.

School Organization and Student Learning

Most children are eager to come to school as kindergartners. They want to know about the things they can play with and what they will learn that older friends and siblings already know. Although school curriculum and requirements align with the developmental social and learning aspects of the human brain, new thinking and higher expectations for rigorous learning have crept into even the early grades. The early school years, too, are being challenged with more comprehensive work. While there were naysayers about an increasingly serious academic curriculum for five- and six-year-olds, children have surprised parents and teachers with their resolve for learning. It turns out the abilities of the young, developing human brain have been underestimated. As the curriculum continues to be more demanding, the children filtering through the school system show capacity to master stronger learning skills and form deeper understanding. This wave of students will defy each ensuing grade-level teacher to provide more challenging learning activities. Learners with higher levels of competence moving through the education system can have exhilarating outcomes.

Another Strong Example

Nothing breeds success like being successful. Sammamish High School (SHS), in Belleview, Washington, lets website viewers know of their success at the first look. SHS among "America's Most Challenging High Schools" greets the reader. Another accolade is that this high school was among *Newsweek*'s list of America's best-100 high schools. On the same first look, those seeking information have quick facts of enrollment, assessment information, attendance area, budget, and even when the campus was renovated, which was in 2004. Fine, but what makes this school stand out from others?

Initially it is learned they have linked with the George Lucas Educational Foundation and the powerful direction identified by STEM (science, technology, engineering, and mathematics). STEM's direction integrates the sciences, all these sciences, into a core focus, giving just as much attention to technology and engineering as formerly was allowed for math and science. It is the brain child from industry with lofty goals for American students by 2020.

Touting a mantra of *our school, our community, our future*, Sammamish High School lives out its vision by partnering also with Washington STEM and the University of Washington Institute of Science and Math Education. Teachers embrace problem-based learning (PBL). An extension of this thinking is extended into a summer program where students work with engineers and other professionals to look at global and local problems. And, yes, there is more support as the Gates Foundation and Valve Software collaborate with this program. While this combination of external financial and resource support is extraordinary and difficult to replicate, others can still seek the root of their success. The key to real learning is what is happening between teachers and students.

Teachers at Sammamish are characterized by their tenacity and connectedness among their colleagues and with both the local and global community. They willingly partner not only with others in the community, but also with their students. It is tricky business to maintain control of the curriculum, be ultimately responsible for student learning, and yet willingly let go of some of the classroom management issues, which incidentally plague classrooms everywhere. At this school, the classroom can be anywhere. For example, several groups from their advanced placement human geography class did research and proposed solutions to agricultural problems in Saharan Africa and South Asia through technology at their school site. Their solutions include new technology, an awareness campaign, and new government policy. Another course, in biology/chemistry, aligned with a research team from the University of Washington to work on a potential cancer drug delivery system. Students work alongside their teachers and STEM professionals in other intensive programs; each one is accomplished in a 7-day institute.

It is a bit overwhelming to think of the way classes are run and the connections that must be in place for a high school that is this dynamic and associates so effectively in the community and in the world. Remember, however, that Sammamish is only 1 of 100 that received recognition by a national magazine, *Newsweek*, in 2013. Other high schools are doing innovative programs that are equally unique and different.

A Brilliant Time to Be in Education

It is amazing to see engineering and technology take their place in the curriculum spotlight. Now students can experience a full range of experiences from the real world and be better prepared for the world they find after graduation. Teachers, through technology, have an endless supply of support and solid lessons for every content area that are based on what has already been successfully done in classrooms worldwide through websites, blogs, and tweets. One such website, http://www.yourchildlearns.com/alpsci.htm, provides active science learning lesson plans and activities for elementary age students. An example, this time for high school, is Share My Lesson by teachers for teachers. This site features all areas of the high school curriculum and is available at http://www.sharemylesson.com/high-school-teaching-resources/. Almost 170,000 different lessons are available and rated.

While these are two examples teachers know they can use Google to look up almost any learning-related request and get real answers instantly from real colleagues. And there is good reason to pull no stops to pursue a new deeper form of learning for students. The Common Core State Standards are roaring into schools with new expectations and an improved outlook for student accomplishments during their school years.

Teaching That
Looks Different

Many schools are well into implementation of the Common Core State Standards. Look in this chapter for ways to infuse brain-based learning techniques to enhance memory skills. Teaching activities that match the rigors of the common core include a new lesson design, a clear look at teacher observation aimed at what students are doing to learn, engaging student activities for advanced learning, and caring about how students feel about school. Here are ideas based on how the human brain is designed to learn that can be used right now.

The Common Core State Standards (CCSS) give educators an opportunity to revolutionize the *how* of teaching, beyond *what* is being learned. Previous reform initiatives have come and gone. Teaching continues to look the same with some variations to the commonly followed lesson plan. As a group of professionals, educators have survived the constant barrage of requirements and changes by systematically following some basic tenants. Beliefs and common practices are hard wired and infused into every teacher's cognitive system, which defines what teachers do at the time of student teaching or internship training. Often the "way of doing teaching" persists throughout a teacher's career. In spite of all the renovations education has experienced, the change efforts themselves have forced educators to seek stability in the basics of the profession. What is happening in many classrooms now *is not so different from what happened when those currently teaching were students themselves.* It is time to upend some current practices and slide in new ones that make more sense according to the way children and young adults learn. The initiation of CCSS provides the right incentives to do just that!

COMMON CORE—WHAT IS SO NEW?

Anyone versed in the buzz about the common core could respond to the question, "What is so new?" Some responses are the inclusion of classroom interaction, inquiry-based approaches, or integration of standards acutely into instruction. Those responses sound reasonable and even comfortable. Others would use expanded descriptions that include instilling a narrow focus for content and coherence across the grades to build on solid foundations that are constructed in the early years. The answer may also be to develop a profound understanding of the content. The new common core standards can best be understood by looking at them for the uniqueness of each for the curriculum areas that have been adopted: Reading, Mathematics, and Science (see Chapter 3).

What is the same about reform initiatives? Every 7 to 10 years there is a new or expanded educational push. Educators have tried strategy-based teaching, basing instruction upon standards, teaching to goals and objectives, and most currently following frameworks and standards for each of the subject matter areas. All the approaches are focused on what the teacher does to cover the curriculum and to act as the change agent for pupils' learning. The constant push is for staff development that helps teachers in their quest to give lessons with expertise. Teachers, their principals, and their coaches all look for instruction that is supported by adequate planning, a lesson design, and a sequence that moves students from awareness to supported practice, to independent work, and culminates with concept and knowledge formation. Ultimately, an assessment is given to determine if students have mastered the desired information.

Prepare Teachers

To do this magnanimous feat of real learning for classrooms of children, massive numbers of teachers attend meetings, seminars, workshops, and conferences. They read volumes of materials and professional books. And they listen to speakers who tell them why the new push in education will yield greater results for more children and students. They engage in study groups and meet for endless hours to plan, coordinate, and analyze test results. They pour over volumes of data sheets to see what they can do differently or more effectively. They continue to take papers home to grade over the weekend and often do their lesson plans Sunday evening, because there is just not enough time to get it done during the work week. Teachers can be found in educational supply stores seeking materials that will stimulate and engage their students, often at their own expense. They seek programs to fortify student learning. Technology is used to keep students focused and interested. And now there is something else, a new thrust to send teachers scrambling. The common core requests new ways of teaching, a new assessment system, and a changed emphasis on what is taught in each grade. It is just one more thing that teachers need to learn about and respond to with altered classroom practices (Petrilli, 2013).

How Teachers Learn to Do What They Do

Teachers are talking. They not only talk with their building colleagues, but they also seek ideas and opinions from a vast number of educators through blogs, educational websites, and social media. One blog addressed the common core as one more demand on teachers' energy, time, and effort. Teachers voice that it is truly impossible to meet all the demands that are placed on them by districts, state government, and the federal education department. There are answers to the how to do the common core question, and some are relatively easy to do.

At recent workshops about learning and the human brain the presenter posed a question. Participants were learning about the different structures in the brain, how they function, and what brain connections and networks have to do with educational practice. Here is the scenario and the question posed to them.

> *You are a part of a school team that has embraced the goal of integrating brain compatible practices into the classroom. Not only are all the teachers in agreement to take this focus into the classroom, but also the principal is supported by the district administration to embrace the concept. To encourage teachers to become well versed in how students learn, your principal offers this opportunity. A list of selected parts of the brain is provided. You are asked to study and learn the names and location of the structures of the human brain and to be able to describe their function. You have one week to study for a short answer test. If you show proficiency by identifying the human brain structures and describing their functions with 90% accuracy, you will be awarded a $1,000 stipend. The funds for the stipend have been approved by the district's school board. The question is, assuming you take the challenge, "How will you study?"*

The participants gave interesting responses. Consider that adults are being asked how they have learned to learn. During the school years, individuals are exposed to various and assorted learning techniques. Students in high school are expected more and more to study on their own. Preferred modes of study emerge for young adults. Sometimes it is expedient to rely on working memory, such as when the individual studies to *pass the test* that is scheduled for tomorrow. Other times the goal is to learn for depth or mastery using long-term memory areas of the brain. By the end of the secondary school system, most young adults have perfected their preferred methods of study. How did this group of adult participants respond with activities that can be useful for classrooms today (see Table 2.1)?

Notice the variety of responses and think about others that are not listed. There are many different variations in the ways adults learn basic information. These differences are greatly influenced by the way the human brain is

Table 2.1 Responses From Adults About Learning Activities

• Make a set of flash cards with the name on the front and the explanation on the back.
• Make a tape recording of the information and play it on my way to work.
• Draw a model of the brain with the parts labeled.
• Read the chapter of a book that describes the brain parts and highlight what I need to remember.
• Write it out in my own words and read it over and over.
• Get a study partner.
• Teach the information to someone else who does not know it.
• Make a diagram and post it to my mirror at home.
• Study the information just before I go to bed at night.
• Practice small bits each day and split up my study time.
• Make up a practice test to give to myself.
• Condense the information onto a small study sheet.
• Simplify the information in a format that my students would understand and teach it to them.
• Switch roles and have my students teach and test me on the information.

built during the childhood years. The examples are simple practices that are geared for the type of learning prior to the CCSS. Innovative common core practices to push further into expansive learning are needed and are described during the course of this book. Professional development specifically designed to immerse teachers into teaching for the common core expectations is addressed in a chapter dedicated to that topic (see Chapter 7).

Learning to Learn

Adults use different strategies to recall something needed for the current day or to really know and remember something necessary for the long term. Often, however, mature learners do not think about how they are learning—they just do it. And, additionally, not only is the process not considered, but adults are also not alert to how much they have learned and what they may not remember (see Chapter 9, Adult Learner Insights).

Teachers know they are responsible for providing a variety of learning and remembering activities for students through practice and rehearsal strategies. Students' learning brains are being developed during childhood. At adulthood the human brain is acutely developed as a thinking and learning organ, designed to serve for a lifetime of learning (see Chapter 9, Adult Brains Designed to Learn). Students everywhere, right now, are having experiences that propel them to construct brains with learning patterns and habits of mind that will work efficiently throughout a lifetime.

School Revolution Supported by Brain Science

A new field called *neuroeducation* is creating a flurry of excitement. For years neuroscientists have discovered more and more fascinating information about human brain function. Neurology initially conducted research to find out about diseases or malfunctions of the human brain. However, in the last 20 years scientists revealed that the human brain is an interesting target for study. They seek clarification about how learning happens because the human brain is far from being rigid. The term *neuroplasticity* was coined (see Chapter 9, Neuroplasticity). Recognize that the human brain is responsive to the environment and continually organizes itself for learning. This known fact matches exquisitely with the requirements of the common core. Our cognitive organ, the human brain, being very impressionable and responsive to change, is the perfect focus for acquiring deep learning. School practices can propel student learning to new levels through acknowledging and partnering with neuroscience.

PREMIUM SCHOOL PRACTICES

Education is embarking on a new era for teaching with common core state level standards. A requirement that students develop deep learning is all over this ambitious effort. It is time to revolutionize how teaching and learning happens with this set of requirements. There are five unique areas of teaching and learning that are attainable, somewhat easy to implement, and provide a different way to *do school.* In this order they are (1) deviate from the traditional step-by-step lesson plan, (2) try something new for student engagement, (3) address students' attitudes about school, (4) revamp the teacher evaluation process, and (5) finally, realize education must embrace brain science now.

The Traditional Lesson Plan

First, consider the 5- or 7-step lesson plan. A step-based lesson plan is taught to pre-service university students. It includes what the teacher will do and what the students will do as an incremental part of lesson planning for student and interim teachers. The lesson design is not only practiced by novice teachers, but is also universally similar to how most experienced teachers are required to design their teaching periods.

It generally involves these or similar steps:

1. Introduce the lesson with an anticipatory set.

2. Let students know what they will be learning.

3. Give students new information with questions scattered into the conversation, maybe include a pair-share.

4. Model some work together.

5. Check for understanding.

6. Send students to work individually or in small groups.

7. Ask students to demonstrate their learning by taking an assessment.

No matter what skill level students need to attain, this sequence or pertinent parts of it are addressed. Most of the teaching profession is committed to this type of overarching lesson plan. Often it is assumed that the lesson plan will fit into one class period. At times it may be extended into the next period, but then teachers risk falling behind and not being able to complete all expected lessons during the grading period.

A New Lesson Plan Design

Some very good thinking has gone into the commonly used lesson plan, and it is conducive to student learning. What needs to be infused is thoughtful planning that goes vertically into the selected context as opposed to covering so many topics at a shallow level. The common core demands this effort. What generally happens is that teachers plan and execute lessons from start to finish as the lesson is designed. There appears to be a lack of agreement among educators over direct instruction versus inquiry-based instruction that is more open-ended. The type of instruction is not an "either-or" proposition. Rather "it depends" on what is being taught. Some standards are learned best by direct instruction, while others are more efficiently learned by extending the time for hands-on exploration and engagement.

Effective teachers continually make decisions during a lesson about how much information students need and how much time they need to be actively engaged with the information. Here is another lesson design for teachers to consider with built-in decision times (see Table 2.2).

This type of questioning is not unlike what effective teachers already do. The decision points here are prompted throughout the lesson plan. Using a design similar to this one makes it alright to spend more time for students to develop a depth of learning. The decision points are critical. Teachers determine how well students are learning, assess if more practice or work time is needed, and make informed decisions based on their knowledge of how students learn. These determinations consider what is happening in the brains of students when they work to master procedures and concepts (see Chapter 9, Practice for Procedures and Concepts).

A Different Teacher Evaluation

Step-by-step lesson planning was challenged, so another bold idea is to look at the way teachers are evaluated. This topic is one that is heatedly discussed at the school and district levels and with departments of education university research teams. Marzano and Toth (2013) wrote an entire book in an attempt to define the characteristics of the next generation of teacher evaluation systems. One key recommendation is that teachers are observed on multiple occasions inside and outside the classroom. This matter is addressed with more detail in Chapter 8. Here the topic is breached to turn perception from what teachers do to what students are doing. The common core standards are written with their focus on student learning. Teachers always remain in control of the design, plan, and preparation of what goes on in the classroom. However, the focus of

Table 2.2 Lesson Planning With Built-In Decision Points

1. **Introduce the topic or concept**. This could happen as a flipped classroom approach where students get initial information as online homework. The introduction could be provided as source material from technology, through students doing problem solving, provided by a provocative story, student development of predictive statements, or be provided by the teacher. (Notice the emphasis on student engagement with the topic right at the onset.)

2. **Give information through a carefully planned method**: direct instruction, technology or Internet resource, or text company-designed format.

3. **Check for student understanding** and probe for misconceptions.

   Decision Point—Do students or groups of students have enough information or competence to work on their own or in groups?

   If yes, proceed.

   If no, continue with input or continued direct instruction or go back to 1 or 2.

4. **Direct students to their next activity** or assignment. Choose the best way for engagement: individual, individual for a defined period of time and then group, partner work, small group, or continue with the whole class. Continually monitor student work. Draw the class back together when many need more background information or skill development.

5. **Draw the whole class together** at appropriate times to give reports on progress.

   Decision Point—Do students understand and are they progressing as anticipated?

   If yes, proceed.

   If no, plan to go back to 1, 2, 3, or 4 during the next class time. Decide if students understand what they are to do, need more time to complete the task, or if they are lacking practice. Possibly, assign additional work for practice or rehearsal as homework, or provide additional class time before Step 6.

6. **Assess student learning.**

   Decision Point—Have students learned this topic to mastery (is mastery needed)? Will they remember it a week from now? Do some students need to be pulled aside for additional practice? Do students need intermittent practice or to revisit this standard again? Is learning adequate for students to draw on it for higher-level projects?

teacher evaluations can be altered to meet the intent of the common core. Consider any combination of these or similar prompts that have a potential to dramatically change the observation perspective from what teachers are doing to what the students are learning.

1. What is being learned?

2. Define the instruction and list supporting information and resources.

3. Describe what is required of students during instruction.

4. How is student learning encouraged, enhanced, and ensured?

6. How are students grouped? (Whole class, large or small groups, work partners, individual.)

7. When is learner attention and engagement most intense?

8. What product or assessment determines the students' level of learning?

Notice the focus on student learning activities; the focus is not on teacher performance. There are benefits to dramatically changing the way we *do school.* It is the responsibility of the education system to direct what students need to learn. Ideally, students have a set of common core standards to learn and understand by the time they exit high school. They can accomplish that feat in an enjoyable, stimulating place called school as they are engaged with learning.

Try Something Different

To honor the well-thought-out common core outcomes, it is time to venture out to practices that have always been attractive but have not been used enough. For starters, consider some of these higher-level learning activities that are already successfully used in some schools (see Table 2.3).

Notice the change of focus. It matters what students are doing—the adults at the school can pick up and be supportive of student behaviors that are learning oriented.

It Matters How Students Feel About School

In a recent focus survey, upper elementary and middle school students were asked what happens in their classrooms. Here are some comments they made about their favorite classes: *my teacher is funny, class is never boring, kids are given a chance to answer questions,* and *each day is pretty different.* Some responses about their least favorite classes were *it's really boring taking notes all the time, we follow the same routine every day, class is monotonous and difficult,* and *my teacher talks a lot and is strict.* The responses from the least favorite class indicate student feelings of apathy, a lack of engagement, and little interest. When students feel like this the emotional center of the brain is understimulated. Learning at this emotional level is minimal; the brain maintains a low level of engagement. The results are just enough learning to "get by," or the brain's neuron stimulation could be high but directed at something more important, even something unrelated to the classroom.

Table 2.3 Challenge Students With Higher-Level Learning Activities

Plan lessons where students are doing most of the work. Allow your class to be a bit more boisterous with the business of learning. Students interact together to **solve problems**, **discuss the reasoning they used, come to common understandings**, and then be capable to **teach the process** to another group of students.

Require students to think differently. Prompt them to **reason abstractly, develop viable arguments** for a process or procedure, and be able to **critique their work** and the work of others.

Change the boundaries for learning. Vary learning activities to include **think sheets; problem of the week; number, word, and concept talk; thinking maps**; and **guessing games**. Request students to make **predictions** about what will be read, and **evaluate** a section or chapter as easy, moderate, or hard before their work. Follow up with **discussion** of their initial thoughts at the conclusion of the work task.

Tap into students' intrinsic motivation by using gaming that aligns with content skills needed. Gaming inherently provides **eye-popping graphics**, assurance there will be **relentless pursuit**, count on **continual progress**, and a rigor for learning that develops from **persistent challenge**.

Challenge students to think, not memorize. Help them use learning strategies that require them to **elaborate and think in pictures**, work with **a giant question**, write **cohesive essays**, deal with **global challenges**, be able to **advocate**, participate on **panel discussions**, and experience all **communication forms**: reading, writing, listening, and speaking.

Provide equity. All students, all the time, are working with challenging work that can lead to successful learning. **Vary the pace, provide extra practice, change the number of requirements, provide alternate resources, give extra support**, all the while maintaining adherence to standards at the grade level of their peers.

Students' attitudes can be detected in the way they talk. Frequently they comment, "I have to go to school." "I can't wait until Saturday or vacation." Also heard is "I'm so bored." School is commonly talked about as a place everyone must go, but almost everyone, teachers and students, would rather to be somewhere else. A kindergartner's excitement to go to school and learn to read can be lost by the end of second grade. Even these young children understand the school routine and realize just what school has been all about—the teacher.

School talk changes when there is a focus on student learning. "I am going to school today" is said with the same tone children use when they say, "We are going to Disneyland!" Or "I can't wait to get to school, because today we are . . . " There are many places where school is being done with the feeling that what is going on at school is important and that school is a fun privilege. Students get to go to school, and teachers get the opportunity to guide what and how students are learning. What conversation is heard at your school?

Neuroscience Provides Answers

Neuroscientists continue to conduct research about brain function and learning that is beneficial to the field of education. Those in education use results from scientific research to answer some of the most intriguing questions.

- Why do some children learn successfully, while others in the same classroom repeatedly fail?
- Why is the information learned on Friday forgotten by Monday?
- What does it really mean to be learning disabled?
- Does heredity or environment have the greatest impact on intelligence?

Thanks to neuroscience, these questions and a barrage of others can begin to be answered (see Chapter 9, Neuroscience Provides Answers). Like the common core expectations, some answers suffice but are not complete. Researchers in neurology continue to gather a richness of understanding as more information is added, more research is completed, and more outcomes are discovered. Information learned from scientific research as well as research from the behavioral sciences has application to the type of learning that is described by the common core.

There are a variety of reasons to initiate a revolutionary changed way to *do school*. Many findings from neuroscience are available for teachers to increase understanding of the neural processes that exist for deep learning. Brain imaging techniques vividly show chemical exchanges and electrical responses in human brains during the very act of learning, as is explained in Chapter 4. Teachers are encouraged to plan classroom practices that excite students, cause explosions among connections in their brains, and help them bind information and concepts into real active learning.

The Common Core Explained in Common Terms

Now is the time to take the mystique out of the common core. It is fascinating to find out why the change in expectations came about and who is pushing for such a dramatic change in outcomes for student learning. This chapter looks at the common core for literacy, mathematics, and science. Teachers can gain new insights and be comfortable with these new requirements for teachers and for students. Those providing educational services are being commandeered to provide a thorough, rigorous education with depth for the subjects selected to study. Expectations boldly demand deeper learning for students in every classroom, at every grade level, and for all types of learners.

Advocates for the Common Core State Standards (CCSS) include business leaders, politicians, educational departments, state governors, and foundations. The common core standards are an improvement from the individual state standards they follow. The common core expectations represent a national effort to address the needs of all the children as they prepare for 21st-century careers and professional positions. In the light of higher order thinking, the previous standards hovered around the knowledge and application levels. In comparison, the common core requires students to achieve at the highest levels of cognitive function, which are characterized by terms like *analysis, concept formation, synthesis,* and *deep understanding*. Students are required, for example, to read with intent, to make logical inferences, and to find and cite textual evidence for their opinions. This huge change in requirements came about with little warning. It rushed in and is accompanied by the development of new assessment systems supported by federal grants.

SOME BASIC INFORMATION

While there is a well-accepted sequence of supports for good educational practice, the common core ignores these expectations. Successful learning happens for students when there is a correlation, or better than that, an explicit match between curriculum standards, text materials, support resources, learner goals and objectives, and the assessment plan (see Table 3.1).

The common core movement provides part of the essential elements, which are well-thought-out standards and a new level of sophistication for assessment. The education system with scattered financial support is left to figure out how to make "it happen." Education is challenged to force a new system of requirements to work with the textbooks and resources that are on hand or are yet to be developed. Teachers rightfully feel anxious. The common core requirements are happening in schools now. Teachers are challenged to make current resources work for an entirely different purpose, and to prepare their students to be assessed at increasingly more intense cognitive levels. The new online assessments students will face are multifaceted, requiring problem solving, and allowing many "right answers" if the logic and level of response is correct. Teachers who have, as recently as the 2012–2013 school year, been requested to teach specific facts and some application skills are now being requested to meet wholly new testing requirements.

Table 3.1 Support System for Student Learning. The first row represents support provided with the previous standards. The second row is the support system for the Common Core State Standards.

Previous Curriculum Standards	Learner Goals and Objectives	Textbooks and Teachers' Guides	Instructional Materials and Resources	Assessments, summative and formative
CCSS Standards and Expectations	To be developed	To be developed	To be developed	Assessments, Summative Formative, to be developed

Know the Players

Many acronyms are used to identify the leaders behind the Common Core State Standards' movement. The ones that are frequently used are demystified with Table 3.2.

Look at Assessments

It may be said that this new push for the common core came about as a matter of economics. Leaders in countries internationally look for favorable test results to determine the success of their nation's schools. Assessments from the Program for International Student Assessment (PISA) and Trends in International Mathematics and Science Study (TIMSS) were reviewed and posted. Basing evaluation of an educational system in a country as large as the United States on numbers and comparisons is a precarious practice. Recently the International Association for the Evaluation of Educational Achievement (IEA) released national average results from tests of mathematics and science. A month later an amended version of the test results was released. Although conclusions from the original report remained the same, the publicly promoted average national results were not initially reported appropriately (Carnoy & Rothstein, 2013).

Educators often rely on reports of this type to make decisions about how funds are expended for education. A 2011 report from the Progress

Table 3.2 Leaders in the Common Core State Standards Are Identified by Initials

Program for International Student Assessment	PISA
Trends in International Mathematics and Science Study	TIMSS
International Association for the Evaluation of Educational Achievement	IEA
Progress in International Reading Literacy Study	PIRLS
Smarter Balanced Assessment Consortium	SBAC
Partnership for Assessment of Readiness for College and Careers	PARCC
Center for Research on Evaluation, Standards, and Student Testing	CRESST
The Business and Industry Science, Technology, Engineering and Mathematics Coalition	STEM
Manpower Demonstration Research Corporation	MDRC

in International Reading Literacy Study (PIRLS) found improvement for United States students from previous tests. Out of 53 participating countries, the United States ranked among the top 13 systems and improved 14 points of 500 in 2011 compared to 2001. Expansive information from recent assessment results and comparisons among the participating countries is available from the Economic Policy Institute (see References and Further Reading).

Common Core Assessment Designers

The Smarter Balanced Assessment Consortium (SBAC or Smarter Balanced) and the Partnership for Assessment of Readiness for College and Careers (PARCC) are the two consortia developing comprehensive, technology-based assessment systems. Assessment of the CCSS will be mandated in the 2014–2015 school year (Herman & Linn, 2013). Educators will have the beginning (the expectations) and the end (the assessment tools). The vital middle parts, alignment of curriculum, teaching, and student activities for learning, are left to be developed. Good educational practice matches curriculum, teaching, learning, and assessment. What is different this time is that deeper learning requires more complex thinking. The goal of all stakeholders is for students to be prepared for an ever changing world with 21st-century skills.

UCLA's National Center for Research on Evaluation, Standards, and Student Testing (CRESST) is monitoring the two consortia's assessment development efforts. The report, funded by the William and Flora Hewlett Foundation, summarizes findings and describes an evidence-centered design assessment framework. As an overseer, it guides assessment development for both Smarter Balanced and PARCC as well as each consortium's plans for system validation. The CRESST report also evaluates the status of deeper learning components that are required to be in both assessment plans.

Other Organizations Have Their Say

Other organizations are also pushing into education's territory, such as the Business and Industry STEM Coalition with its ambitious goal to double the number of graduates with a bachelor's degree in science, technology, engineering, or mathematics (STEM) between 2010 and 2020. The coalition includes more than 40 business and industry associations and states,

The Business and Industry STEM Coalition announced its commitment to doubling the number of graduates with a bachelor's degree in science, technology, engineering or mathematics (STEM) to 400,000 from 200,000 by 2020. (Dador & Bommelje, 2010)

Organizations, such as Manpower Demonstration Research Corporation (MDRC), launched by the Ford Foundation, aim to document projects that evaluate programs from preschool through twelfth-grade education and include higher education. Big business, government, and policy institutes are all over education. These giants and their expansive resources loom over state and local education agencies. It is no wonder there is so much pressure to "get it right" in classrooms everywhere.

Education and getting it right is so important that the United States Department of Education used its signature, Race to the Top, to put grant money totaling $400 million into school organizations. The recipients represent traditional districts, charter districts, and educational cooperatives. They differ immensely in the ways they are making over schools and classroom experiences. Collectively those awarded grants utilize similar, familiar responses, such as individualized learning plans, data dashboards for collecting student learning data, technology and mobile devices, and learning coaches for teachers (McNeil, 2013).

Deeper Learning Defined

The Hewlett Foundation (2013) provides leadership and support to the current educational movement by signifying five markers that are significant for students to develop deep learning (see Table 3.3).

Notice the emphasis on thinking, learning, and academic mindsets. Educational practice is guided toward learning, learning as the outcome of the teaching process. Again, the focus is on deep thinking. The education system is requested to teach students to learn how learning happens. This feat cannot be done well without understanding how the learning organ, the brain, functions. The era of the human brain and learning has patiently waited for a debut. The time is finally here.

Table 3.3   Markers of Deep Learning

- Master core academic content.
- Think critically and solve complex problems.
- Work collaboratively.
- Learn how to learn.
- Develop academic mindsets.

Next-Generation Assessments and Bloom's Taxonomy

The two consortia developing the assessments for the common core represent multiple states. Students will be taking the next-generation assessments online. Problems they will be requested to solve represent the higher order thinking skills of analysis and synthesis. Some parts of the assessment process require students to search the Internet for information, to take a substantiated stand on a critical issue, evaluate arguments, and write powerful statements about what they have learned. The cognitive level is quite different from what students have experienced, even struggled with in the past. Assessment of this type requires very different classroom activities to prepare students to produce at this level. A step back in time allows educators to revive a standard teaching and learning tool from the past, Bloom's Taxonomy.

Blooms Taxonomy, developed by Benjamin Bloom in the 1950s, may be remembered by teachers from their university training as beginning teachers. Table 3.4 uses a fourth-grade standard to show lower levels of learning for memory and recall and how thinking becomes more complex with a simple task. Higher levels require putting information from different sources into an amalgamated product and evaluating the outcome.

Teachers are required to prepare students for a new order of testing by providing a new order of learning. The key to this transformation is for teachers to understand how their students learn most effectively by getting connected with what neurology tells us about how students learn. The new

Table 3.4   Example: CCSS.ELA-Literacy.RL.4.5 Explain major differences between poems, drama, and prose, and refer to the structural elements of poems (e.g., verse, rhythm, meter) and drama (e.g., casts of characters, settings, descriptions, dialogue, stage directions) when writing or speaking about a text (Reading Literature, Grade 4).

Knowledge: Give a definition for poem, drama, and prose.
Comprehension: Match the term poem, drama, or prose to a descriptive definition.
Application: Find an example of a poem, a drama, and prose.
Analysis: Give the structural elements of poems, drama, and prose from samples provided and discuss them with your partner or small group.
Evaluation: Write an essay to explain the major differences between poems, drama, and prose.
Synthesis: Select one of the literary types to write a short (1–2 pages) example. Be certain to include the structural elements listed in the definition. Prepare to read your product to the class and identify examples of the elements.

standards for the common core shout for an understanding of how students can learn to learn. Chapters following this one provide information about classroom activities to help students learn about learning.

THE COMMON CORE STANDARDS IN COMMON LANGUAGE

The standards hold a vision and message of what is expected from a literate person in the 21st century with wide application to areas that extend beyond the classroom. They are designed to equip students for deep understanding of written works and to enjoy complex literature. Students under the common core standards prepare to critically read large volumes of information that is available in print and digitally. Cogent reasoning skills paired with ability to search for powerful evidence will allow today's students as citizens in the 21st century to deliberate and evaluate information presented to them and to act responsibly in a democracy.

Standards are available for Literacy, Mathematics, and Science at this printing. Each subject is presented next with its unique qualities and expectations. Look first at some examples that compare the previous standards and the common core at three grade levels and for the three different content areas (Table 3.5).

COMMON CORE FOR LITERACY

The common core for literacy addresses reading, writing, speaking, and listening and is called ELA: English, Language Arts. The ELA standards cluster around three main ideas:

1. text-based answers to reading comprehension questions,

2. source-based writing, and

3. academic vocabulary.

Student activities look very different as the focus turns to communication skill building. Students are asked to share findings, conduct research, assimilate information from vast resources, evaluate, and synthesize. Rather than a printed or online textbook, they are lead to use print and nonprint texts from a variety of media sources, which could be old or new. New to this educational scene are the ever present requirements of conducting research and accessing media. These elements are embedded as communication activities throughout the standard expectations.

Table 3.5 Comparison of Previous and Common Core Standards

Previous Standards	*Common Core Standards*
Reading/Language Arts (First Grade)	
Concepts about Print—1.1: Match oral words to printed words, 1.2: Identify the title and author of a reading section. 1.3: Identify letters, words, and sentences. Narrative Analysis of Grade-Level–Appropriate Text—3.1: Identify and describe the elements of plot, setting and character(s) in a story, as well as the story's beginning, middle, and ending (Reading/Language Arts Framework for California Schools, p. 69).	CCSS.ELA-Literacy.W.1.1: Ask and answer key questions about key details in a text. 1.2: Identify main topic and key details of a text. 1.3: Describe the connections between two individuals, events, ideas, or pieces of information in a text. 1.5: Know and use various text features (e.g. headings, tables of contents, glossaries, electronic menus, icons) to locate key facts or information in a text (Common Core Standards for Literacy/ELA).
Math (Sixth Grade)	
Number Sense—1.1 compare and order positive and negative fractions, decimals, and mixed numbers and place them on a number line. The ordering of fractions is best done through the use of the cross-multiplication algorithm, which says . . . Of particular importance is the students' understanding of the positions of the negative numbers and the geometric effect the numbers of the number line when a number is added or subtracted from them (Mathematics Frameworks for California Public Schools, p. 160).	The Number System—Apply and extend previous understandings of multiplication and division to divide fractions by fractions. 1. Interpret and compute quotients of fractions, and solve word problems involving division of fractions by fractions, e.g., by using visual fraction models and equations to represent the problem. *For example, create a story context for $(2/3) \div (3/4)$ and use a visual fraction model to show the quotient; use the relationship between multiplication and division to explain that $(2/3) \div (3/4) = 8/9$ because $3/4$ of $8/9$ is $2/3$. (In general, $(a/b) \div (c/d) = ad/bc$.) How much chocolate will each person get if 3 people share 1/2 lb of chocolate equally?* (Common Core Math Standards for Sixth Grade, p. 2).
Science (Grades Nine through Twelve)	
Atomic and Molecular Structure—1. The periodic table displays the elements in increasing atomic number and shows how periodicity of the physical and chemical properties of the elements relates to atomic structure. As a basis for understanding this concept: a. Students know how to relate the position of an element in the periodic table to its atomic number and atomic mass (Science Framework for California Public Schools, p. 186).	HS-PS1–2: Construct and revise an explanation for the outcome of a simple chemical reaction based on the outermost electron states of atoms, trends in the periodic table, and knowledge of the patterns of chemical properties (Next Generation Science Standards, Appendix G, p. 5).

Teachers are required to prepare students to independently read high volumes of complex information from a variety of content areas. An increasing emphasis on informational text is inherent. Informational versus literary text requires increasing informational text from 50% of the reading in fourth grade to 55% by eighth grade. The requirement culminates with a requirement that 70% of the text provided is expository by twelfth grade. These percentages are consistent with the National Association of Educational Progress (NAEP) requirements for literacy. An NAEP document released in 2012 gives a summary of findings for assessments given to fourth-, eighth-, and twelfth-grade students.

Deeper Learning for ELA

The common core ELA standards expect students to be able to explain, persuade, and convey experiences beginning with the elementary years. By sixth grade the standards are defined in two sections, the first being English/Language Arts, while the second part addresses history/social science, science, and technical subjects. Notice the integration of core areas across the curriculum. The expectation is that by twelfth-grade students will be able to participate in a task representing a variety of interrelated content areas to demonstrate critical thinking.

Participating in a task to demonstrate critical thinking begins with students performing close reading of complex, selected literary works all representing a related genre. They may be directed to respond to a "giant question." To complete the task learners must show their thinking, as they critically analyze or compare the selected resources, and come to an informed conclusion. Their response most likely will expand further as they talk with others in their class or outside the classroom. Not only is there a giant question to answer, but this type of deep learning and responding also takes a massive amount of gainfully engaged student work. Teachers are required to think and plan for long-term projects that allow time for this level of thinking to develop.

What Literacy Standards Do Not Address

The standards are expectations that must be complemented by a well-developed, content-rich curriculum. Teachers are not told how to teach, rather what is expected from students when they are at certain checkpoints and at high school exit. The common core articulates fundamentals. Curriculum designers and teachers are challenged to develop the content. No definition is given for advanced work nor is it defined how interventions and additional supports or accommodations should be available for students who are not able to attain the required proficiencies.

COMMON CORE FOR MATHEMATICS

This set of expectations has fewer topics than the previous mathematic standards, but the topics that are selected radiate more depth and rigor. Specific topics are assigned to grade levels or blocks. There is coherent movement of skills from *simple to complex* and *complex to advanced* through the grade levels. A research approach based on the development of students' mathematical knowledge, skill, and understanding is designed to unfold over the school years. Students at each age level must understand mathematical concepts so well that they can justify why a particular math statement is true. Tasks such as these require students to use and understand procedural skills and to be able talk through their responses. This level of answer demands a sufficient richness to show understanding.

The common core for mathematics is noted for what it does not include: long lists of topics that could not possibly be covered in a single year. According to Robert Rothman (2012) the common core is intended to have a **greater focus** on fewer topics so students can develop a real understanding of them. Some topics are missing or not presented until later grades. The calendar is not included at all. Think about the time in an elementary classroom that is spent on the calendar. Will it remain as an ELA activity? Interestingly, data and statistics first appear in the sixth grade. Number sense, which is considered a very important topic, receives considerably more attention than it has in the past. It is the foundation for more advanced topics.

Each grade level has new topics, as previous ones have been developed with depth. This **coherence** suggests relationships between students' understanding of one topic as a foundation for the next one. For example, to understand ratio and proportion, a learner must have an understanding of equations. There is greater emphasis on mathematic practices with specific criteria (see Table 3.6).

Clear sign posts for mathematical development during the years are provided. The goal is to prepare students during their school years to be capable college students and for success in career positions. Standards for all grades identify each teaching domain with specific content descriptors. Gone are the teaching days where students memorize a set of steps, apply them to a problem, and check the correctness of the answer. The common core expects students to conquer skills for each successive year and to move to higher levels. Learners need to show competency with number

Table 3.6   Mathematic Practices in the Common Core State Standards

Making sense of problems
Being persistent to solve them
Reasoning abstractly and quantitatively
Selecting appropriate tools
Strategically deciding on process
Constructing viable arguments for one's work
Critiquing the reasoning of others (Rothman, 2012)

operations, to understand how an answer is found, what it means, and to be able to communicate the process.

> In math, the shift is away from lectures and rote working of equations to the practical application of mathematical processes, often in teams, to real-world situations. Students might use probability to make decisions, geometry to design a bridge, and statistics to create surveys. (Gearson, 2012, p. 1)

One educator who is providing encouragement to those faced with this massive change in thinking and learning is Dan Meyer. This high school math teacher has become a celebrity of sorts because he gives the real deal of how mathematics has been taught in the past. He describes students who lack initiative, are unwilling to persevere, and who avoid word problems with a preference for applying a formula. He paints very different possibilities as he redefines a math curriculum designed to make sense of the world. He speaks of mathematics that uses multimedia and piques students' intuition. He encourages teachers to begin by asking short questions and letting the students build the problems. Teachers are encouraged to use materials that are less helpful (no answers at the back of the book), and use math and science to serve conversations, not conversations serving math. Think about it; the formulation of the problem provides the potential for deeper thinking. One of Meyer's many YouTube videos is described like this:

> Today's math curriculum is teaching students to expect—and excel at—paint-by-numbers classwork, robbing kids of a skill more important than solving problems: formulating them. In his talk,

Dan Meyer shows classroom-tested math exercises that prompt students to stop and think. (Filmed at TEDxNYED [http://www.ted.com/tedx/events/223].)

Mr. Meyer talks about building the brain's neural pathways with problems that decode life. Certainly, teachers must understand what happens in the human brain for learners to develop curiosity and urgency. It is a learner's urgency that propels them to use computation and math processes to define the world around them.

NEXT GENERATION SCIENCE STANDARDS

Notice a slight change in the standards for science education. The title is Next Generation Science Standards (NGSS). This set of expectations for science education is reflective of the interconnectedness of science to the real world. Like the new mathematics standards, the hope is for students to actively engage in scientific and engineering practices to deepen their understanding in these fields. The standards call for the application of "cross cutting concepts." Students are at the center of three dimensions: science and engineering practices, cross cutting concepts, and disciplinary core ideas.

Cross-cutting concepts in curriculum could be patterns, cause and effect, stability or change. The terms mentioned in the standards are close to the way the human brain likes to work. It is a pattern-seeking organ. Students' brains function best on information that is logical; the human brain is constantly unconsciously seeking stability. When change from the norm is detected, the brain rapidly seeks to adjust to the changes and to become stable once again. Interestingly, standards for science education are in alignment with the science of learning.

The standards are not a science curriculum. Rather they are well designed learning progressions. Their intent is to interconnect ideas over a period of time using specific learning processes (see Table 3.7).

Educational supports and experiences must be designed to provide a coherent progression that is aimed at overall scientific literacy. This feat is achieved in small sets of ideas that build on what is needed at the next grade band beginning in the middle school years. Engineering and technology receive the same attention as science has in the past. In addition to scientific inquiry, students are expected to engage in engineering design and exploration with the use of technology. By integrating the core ideas from engineering and technology, the content of science will be more reflective of daily life and allow students to tackle world problems that are a part of 21st-century living (Gross, 2013).

Table 3.7   Next Generation Science Standards Learning Processes

Understand and apply
Employ scientific inquiry and engineering design
Intertwine knowledge and practice
Use models to represent or describe
Predict, collect data, and analyze

More Scientists, Engineers, and Mathematicians Needed

The United States is not producing enough college and high school graduates with an interest in the fields of science, engineering, or mathematics. The Hechinger Report (Stainburn, 2011) revealed that 65% of current scientists and science graduate students developed their interest in science prior to middle school, not in high school. It was argued that present science classes feature too many disconnected subjects without depth. Science classes most often require students to memorize facts rather than promoting understanding of scientific process through inquiry-based instruction. As a result of an education that requires little engagement, science students lack curiosity and show a dulled sense of wonder. The school system has encouraged its students to have lazy habits of mind. They are likely to want the teacher to tell them what to learn rather than being encouraged to put in the necessary time and brain effort into independent learning at deep levels of understanding.

Our federal education focus generally has not promoted scientific study or discoveries as nationally important topics. This lack of influence is another reason science has not been selected for future study by a significant number of secondary school students. Science has simply not received high attention from local, state, or federal educational systems or enough feature articles from the Associated Press. Instead science has been portrayed to the public as an area fraught with controversial topics, such as global warming and evolution versus creation.

Questionable Reviews of the NGSS

The Next Generation Science Standards are not without faultfinders. A recent report from the Fordham Foundation gives the standards a grade of "C." The following criticisms are noted:

1. Practices are not feasible or worthwhile.

2. Prerequisite content is omitted that would prepare students for physics and chemistry.

3. It is assumed that students have mastered prerequisite content that is not spelled out in the standards.

4. "Assessment boundaries" are incorporated that are meant to limit the scope of knowledge and skills, but actually are likely to limit curriculum, especially for advanced students.

5. Math content that is critical for learning science is limited. (Gross, 2013)

When the current standards for science were reviewed by the Fordham Foundation on a state-by-state basis, as many as 16 states received a failing grade. Only 5 of the 50 states received an "A" score. Seven states could boast a "B" rating, while 22 received "C" and "D" scores. All in all, both present and proposed science standards are falling short of expectations to prepare students for careers and college (Finn & Porter-Magee, 2013).

What Is Still Needed?

Adopting expectations for student learning is the first step, but implementation of these new standards is in the infancy stages for many. Still needed are curriculum with aligned instructional materials, completion of strong assessment tools for formative as well as summative evaluations, and educator retooling to equip them to teach the standards with passion and purpose. There is a glaring absence of parent and care provider involvement. District and building plans need to be developed for family understanding and involvement with the common core. Finally, although special educators (education teachers) participated in the development of CCSS, students who require special services are not adequately addressed in any one of the three defined subject areas. To arm teachers with *an understanding of how learning comes about* for all students has the potential to propel these lofty expectations for success in the classrooms around the nation.

How Learning Happens

4

As it happens the common core standards are just the right push for education and its students. In the last few years, we learned that students are actually capable of more learning and more understanding, even at the earliest grades. What is this miraculous learning organ called the human brain that allows such feats? How hard can we push students to develop good habits of mind? At many schools we are just touching the surface of what our students are capable of doing with our present approaches to learning. With the common core standards come instructional shifts that mean an overhaul of the school system. Let's get it right.

The *mysterious black box*, a term some people use to identify the human brain, is no longer a secret. Neuroscientists are discovering, scientists are sharing, and teachers are listening. Teaching practices can be more dynamic and more intense when they shift to what the student is learning and move away from how teachers perform to instruct. Remember those who are doing the most talking are most likely the ones who are doing the most learning.

LEARNING ABOUT LEARNING

The human brain weighs about three pounds and is a mass of structures, connections, and nerve cells. It is protected by fluids and a bony skull. Some brains are bigger than others, but size is not reflective of its capabilities. The important measure of the brain is how quickly the parts of the brain connect to each other and are organized for learning and remembering. The outside world, including the time spent in school, influences individuals' brains to establish what they learn in logical patterns and to make strong connections among the structures that can be accessed and reported at a whim.

Basic Brain Structures

Some basic structures are of importance and interest to teachers. Mostly, it is known that there are two hemispheres and each side has a twin set of what is available on the other side. The two parts of the brain are connected by a heavy bundle of fibers, the *corpus callosum*. The connection allows communication between the more sensitive right brain and the logical left brain as a person makes decisions. There are special structures, called lobes, to receive and interpret information from the senses, for vision, listening, touch, smell, and taste. The limbic or primitive section of the brain responds unconsciously to threats and opportunities, and a centrally located structure, the *thalamus*, sends input from the senses to specially designed areas for association and meaning. All the areas that identify sensory input and translate it into recognizable information are located in the outermost heavily folded layers of the brain called the *cerebral cortex*. See Figures 9.1 and 9.2 for locations of the structures of the cerebral cortex.

The marvelously designed brain also has special bands, the *sensory cortex*, often called the *somatosensory cortex*, and *motor cortex* to coordinate input from the senses and to be able to activate the muscles of the body to respond appropriately. These strips for sensory input and motor response are located like headbands across the top of the brain from ear to ear. At times people respond unconsciously, because the limbic center responds to a threat, but most of the time people make conscious decisions to move. They do not have to concentrate on coordinating the motions of movement. For example, a student is asked to place a comment on a chart. The student response is to get up and move to the area. This feat happens without thinking about how to walk and move but with conscious attention to placing the comment on the chart.

The Site of Working Memory

The *hippocampus* is a structure buried in the limbic system. As the source of working memory, it has the ability to work with information that is consciously practiced. Once something has been practiced enough, the brain unconsciously relocates the information, idea, concept, or practice to other areas of the *cerebral cortex* for long-term memory storage. For example, a student has studied the effects of the railroad system on the development of the Western United States. The information gleaned may be stored in the visual association area for how the trains and their patterns of tracks looked. An association in the auditory area may relate how the steam engine and railroad signals sounded. The *olfactory area* may be activated by the thoughts of how the smoke clogged the passengers' nostrils. The *frontal lobes*, the executive function area of the brain, might be activated to compare the difference between the progress achieved by the development of the railroad system versus the outcome of travel that resulted from the introduction of automobiles. Many areas of the brain can be activated for one complex thought.

While it is not necessary for teachers to become neuroscientists to be effective as learning facilitators, it is important for them to know what works for students to make the most of the time they spend in school. It is during the school years that the human brain is organized and structured for a lifetime of learning. How students learn to learn is of ultimate importance. See Chapter 9, Basic Brain Structures, for each of the brain parts given in this section.

The Sensory Input System

Everyone knows humans have five senses. The commonly known senses—seeing, hearing, touching, and tasting—are not fully developed at birth and complete their wiring in the brain in the first couple of years to become fully functional. The sense of smell is ready to receive and respond to stimulation when a child is born, as it is a survival issue. Infants need to be able to seek comfort and food from their environment, and mom has a recognizable smell. But not everyone realizes that if humans did not have any senses the world and everything in it would be unknown. Nothing would be available to stimulate the brain. The brain develops because it receives input from the environment and learns to interpret the stimulation to make sense out of the world.

Knowing that, it is easy to realize that every single person has unique, individual information that is received by the brain to be processed by the brain. As the brain eagerly accepts input from the world around it, it figures out how to store information. If something regularly or even erratically reoccurs as input to the brain, it is more likely to be recorded and can be recalled for some kind of response beginning at a very early age.

Often people think that babies do not remember anything from their earliest months, but they do. A baby may not recall a traumatic experience to talk about it, but it is recorded in the emotional center of the brain, the limbic system. Although babies come into the world with a certain inherited temperament, their complete emotional self is greatly influenced by their environment. Although the language system is not developed for them to remember in words from the first years, the emotional system does not need words to remember. So even parents are sometimes baffled by emotional responses of their children. Each is so unique and at times is not able to tell why a certain reaction, either of fright or pleasure, is so prominent.

With the continual input of information, the human brain needs to focus on what is important for survival. When the emotional and physical needs are at homeostasis, attention can be given to other input, such as what is being learned at school. Therefore, if something traumatic happened in the morning at home (i.e., there is no breakfast, or a child is sick), attention is focused on that deficiency. Teachers and schools in general provide for these situations.

> If food is not available at home—provide it at school.

> If the child is experiencing trauma from home—provide nurture and support.

> If a child is sick—home is the best place to be.

> If there are problems with peers—thoroughly deal with it.

> If a student is a poor reader—reading out loud in front of peers is not an option.

Issues such as these must receive attention. A human brain can only focus on one thing at a time. Personal problems must be resolved if thinking is expected for learning to occur.

Filtering Systems

The human brain is equipped with filtering systems. Some students have better systems than others, and they are able to concentrate on the topic at hand with relative ease. Others may need to work at maintaining their attention but are able to control their thinking. The number of students with a diagnosis of attention deficit hyperactivity disorder (ADHD) is relatively small. Children with this disorder may have behavior plans or take medication. They have connectivity and chemical irregularities that disrupt their filtering systems and make it difficult or nearly impossible to stay with an academic task without some intervention. See Chapter 9 for more information on Filtering Systems and for new information about ADHD.

The brain's filtering systems allow most of the unimportant input from the senses to drop away, not to be realized by the brain as it is engaged with more important work. The sound of the air conditioning system or a classmate dropping a pencil is noticed slightly but not with enough importance to disrupt focus from the learning activity. This filtering happens in the brain's limbic system and happens unconsciously. Another filtering system occurs because the learner consciously decides the information is not important enough to spend any thinking time on it. In this case the frontal lobes and basal ganglia are involved.

As surely as information comes into the brain, a student is motivated to do something with it. A critical change can happen in schools with student output activities. Often the output system for learners is to respond to questions posed by the teacher, write answers on a worksheet, or take notes. With the wave of precise new expectations from the common core educators can look at a vast array of additional options. Basically, teachers can talk less, while students are encouraged to talk more. Students must have the opportunity to activate their brains with the information that is to be processed and remembered. There are rich arrays and avenues teachers can select to keep track of and assess students learning, which are explored with depth in the next chapter.

Neuroplasticity

An exciting piece of information from neuroscience is that the brain continues to change itself throughout life in response to the environment of the brain's owner. Changing itself means that the connections among the structures of the brain can be minimal or exceptionally strong based on what is happening around the individual. As input is received a student both consciously and unconsciously decides to pay attention or to ignore the received signals. When a conscious decision is made to think about the input there is a greater chance that the information will be remembered. And the result in the brain is a strengthening of reactions among the nerve cells, the neurons. Neuron pathways between different structures of the brain where information is stored can be difficult to access when they are minimally used, but those pathways that are frequented through learning engagement respond swiftly.

Through the course of childhood, the brain's response to its environment literally builds learning capabilities. Children from homes and schools where they are exposed to rich language, interesting situations, and are challenged to investigative inquiry develop brains that not only respond to, but also seek constant stimulation. The brain logically organizes itself to respond to the situations that are commonly experienced. Heredity through gene arrangement plays an inherent part of the structures that compose the human brain. But neuroplasticity rules the construction of the way the brain functions during the childhood and adolescent years.

Stimulating Classrooms

Students are fortunate when they are in classrooms where they are challenged to organize, sort, match, distinguish, connect, condense, discover, and analyze, for example. These tasks assist the brain as it subconsciously labors to place information, ideas, and concepts into efficient storage areas. Some examples of classroom activities that support the learning brain are provided.

- Find the words that *describe* and those that are *nouns.* Make a list of each.
- Take the new vocabulary words and make three lists: *words unknown to me, words I somewhat know,* and *words I need to study.*
- Use these two reading selections. Find similarities and dissimilarities of the writing style of each author.
- Seek anything you can find about a new topic of study before tomorrow's class (following a brief introduction of the study).
- Ask five other students to tell you one thing learned from this week's study. Each response must be unique. Write the responses and a comment about each.

The development of logical storage areas for recall, which develop during the school years, becomes somewhat hard wired. It becomes the system that is in place for all the years of learning as an adult. Adults continue to learn, and their brains continue to respond to the environment and to change with new ideas and information, but the system or process that is accessed for learning remains the same as what was formed during childhood.

MEMORY SYSTEMS

The school system relies on students' memory systems to assess student learning. Students are often required to respond with short, factual answers, which most likely come from one location in the brain. Other complex prompts require them to access memory from several different areas of the brain. While recall and remembering is attributed to a phe-nomenon referred to as *memory*, it is important to understand there is more than one memory system. The memory systems in the human brain are not isolated areas, rather information, concepts, and occurrences that are stored in many places for many reasons.

Procedural Memory

The fact that children access their memory instantaneously on a regular basis is no small feat. It requires the brain to use different memory systems. One is called *procedural memory*. It is part of the nondeclarative memory system that develops in the brain through practice and repetition. A vivid example is seen as an infant learns to crawl. It takes so many times for the little one to push, pull, straighten, lift, and rock before it all comes together and a crawling movement results. This accomplishment is a major developmental feat. All the antics that lead up to it are the child's brain's way of training itself to direct movement of the body and limbs. After much practice, the movements become automatic in procedural memory. The child has mastered crawling.

Reading is a procedural memory process. Unlike learning to crawl, learning to read with mastery takes many years. It begins in early child-hood as infants, toddlers, and preschoolers are exposed to the sounds of language. Parents and care providers are encouraged to talk, talk, talk to their little ones. Almost like magic children learn the rules of oral language and begin to speak. They learn so well in an environment that is rich in language that by the time they reach kindergarten they can under-stand what is being told to them. Five-year-olds are able to answer ques-tions in semantically correct sentences. All this happens with relative ease for most children. It is an automatic process that the human brain is designed to accomplish through procedural memory.

The reading process begins with a strong oral language system. In school children have to be taught and learn to read; it does not happen naturally. However, each child is equipped with a human brain that has all the struc-tures needed for reading (see Chapter 9, Pathways for Reading). To be precise, a child uses the same pathway for reading as was used for speaking with some slight deviations. During the course of the preschool, kindergarten, and first-grade years, children learn to co-opt the oral language route for speaking into doubling as a decoding pathway for reading. Once that pathway is easily accessed and well-developed, children are able to read with fluency and auto-maticity by the malleable design of the procedural memory system.

Although much struggle and thought goes into learning to read with fluency, the child is not consciously aware of the skirmishes that go on in brain. It is tough work, but the results are worthwhile. The procedural memory system capably handles the job. Once a child learns to read, word identification happens spontaneously. A new, more efficient route is used in the brain that does not have so many stop signs for analysis of words (see Chapter 9, Pathways for Reading).

Semantic Memory

Word identification is the introductory part of reading. According to the Common Core Reading and Language Arts Standards, strong foundations need to be built and then expanded on with higher level skills. And that is exactly what reading programs do in schools everywhere. Reading comprehension uses *semantic memory*. This part of the declarative memory system allows students to expand and maintain general information about the world based on their experiences. Children learn by active physical engagement and by involvement with reading.

Each child is exposed to different experiences, and the human brain is designed to remember what is important to the individual. Everyone has a different schematic for the information that is stored in the brain and how it is organized. The brain's organization depends on day-to-day experiences. No two children, even identical twins, form the same associations or networks of ideas. Consequently, no two have the same information in their semantic memories.

Continuing with the reading topic, it is known that semantic memory gives meaning to what is read or experienced. Actually learning to identify and say words in reading is the easy part and can be taught quite systematically. But learning to comprehend is a dicey process. That complex process happens in the upper elementary years and continues throughout a person's life. During the school years, students are continually exposed to a variety of courses they take and various virtual or real-life experiences. All this sensory stimulation is important to gain access to semantic memory. This system allows one to store core information that can be recalled in an instant and applied to the topic at hand during reading, listening, writing, or having conversation. Learning to read becomes a sensational progressive feat, accomplished with more and more complexity. Learning to read with automaticity and comprehension is a prime example of the rigorous teaching requested by the Common Core State Standards.

Other Memory Systems

Reading and learning in general are not processes that can be minimized into simply procedural and semantic memory systems. There are other aspects of memory that come into play. Previously, it was stated that information is stored in memory from experiences. There is a special declarative memory system for remembering information from emotional and active involvement. It is called *episodic memory*. Unlike semantic memory which is gained in a somewhat systematic way, episodic memory can happen at any time and generally has an emotional base. The more the emotional center of the brain is activated, the less accurate the memory will be (see Chapter 9, Emotional System).

For example, a field trip for a class of 30 students is recapped and remembered as 30 different and unique experiences, even though all the students went on the same trip at the same time. Episodic memory is working overtime and will be recorded and remembered differently for each traveler. A teacher can plan to overcome the inefficiency of episodic memory by directing the information to be learned. A hook is needed to activate semantic memory rather than the emotional areas of the brain. Semantic memory can be stimulated by giving students an assignment to record words or pictures to respond to focusing questions. This list gives some questions that could be given prior to the trip:

- Make a list of different words you heard that need to be explained.
- List each new idea you had during the trip.
- What was the most startling thing you learned?
- What else do you want to know?
- What did you already know that was strengthened by this experience? Explain how.
- Would you suggest that another class visit this place? Why or why not?

The follow-up to an adventure like a field trip is the focused learning part of the experience, which is prompted prior to the trip and directed after the experience.

Episodic memory can be tamed and become a worthy tool to address during a unit of study. Students' brains are easily activated during other engaging activities, such as having a guest speaker, acting out a scenario, using artifacts, capturing the concept by cartoons, or doing an experiment. A well-designed activity accompanied by an emotional experience is especially purposeful when it transfers to semantic memory for accurate recording and remembering.

Rote Memory and Drill Practices

A final look at memory begs for an understanding of the second type of memory that is nondeclarative, *rote memory*. Recently, the practice of drilling repetitiously for information to be remembered has been criticized.

It has been called "drill and kill," and rightfully so, if it is used to remember things that need to be experienced to be remembered as semantic memory. Items for semantic memory are best learned through elaborative practice and activities.

However, some things are learned best through repetitive practice. They are, for example, sight words, which need to be taught separately from decodable words. Sight words do not follow the rules of phonics, and they do not look like they sound. Children effectively learn these hard to remember words through practice and drill. Math facts and names of persons, places, and things are other examples of items that are practiced until they can be stored in rote memory for instant recall. Flashcards and other types of instant recall activities are effectively used for these hard to remember pieces. In a recent blog, one educator vied to include rote memorization of poetry. Do it, he proposed, to accept the challenge, exercise the brain, and gain new insights such as assonance, alliteration, and word analogies.

One last comment about memory relates to decodable words. Once a word is sounded out many times, it too becomes a part of rote memory. How many times it needs to be practiced depends on many aspects of each child's developing brain. Everyone is different. Rote memory coupled with procedural memory is exceptionally active during reading. Memory systems, declarative and nondeclarative are further explained in Chapter 9.

Deep Learning and Inner Connectivity

Beyond the visible structures of the brain are the micro parts where the action takes place. Infinitesimally tiny nerve cells, *neurons*, with their even smaller brain cells, *glial cells*, control the actions of the brain during thinking. Information from neuroscience again prompts understanding of the thinking and learning process. Although the number of neurons remains relatively the same, except when neurogenesis happens to birth new neurons, it is not the sheer number of neurons that intrigue educators. What happens during learning, the increase in numbers of connections, is impressive. The denser the network of connections is, the richer the learning is about that topic. Learners unconsciously build explosive neuron networks when they consciously engage with learning activities, such as these (see Chapter 9, Neuron Networks):

- Build a model that exemplifies the concepts you have learned.
- Collaborate with a peer group via the Internet to finalize your essay.
- Check with five peers to validate your response by signing their names.

- Develop a written summary with your small group that reflects not only the group's decision, but also the process you used to agree.
- Attend and evaluate at least three presentations provided by our grade level.
- Plan a presentation to present at least three times to various grade level peers.
- Be prepared to be on a panel to represent either side of this issue.

Intense student attention and engagement yield learning with rich attributes. Students who do not pay attention and give minimal effort to engage in learning opportunities end up with minimal or nonexistent learning for the intended topic. Decisions for teaching and learning activities based on this information from brain science can help those in education reach the high expectations brought to schools by the common core.

So Many Ways to Learn: What Teachers Are Doing

How it looks, sounds, and feels in classrooms where learning is the goal and students are the object of all that happens. This chapter contains a bold new way for teachers to plan through a series of challenging questions. The focus is on what students will be doing during learning. Bringing students into the process of their own learning is what education can be all about.

Teachers are taking hold of the common core expectations in a bold way. They are the ones who are the force behind all education. Educators are intelligent; they are knowledgeable. They love students and are capable of providing the best education possible for them. This group could decide to shirk from the new lofty expectations expressed by the Common Core State Standards (CCSS), but they are embracing them. Teachers know this new direction is right for the nation's students. They are ready to fight and unite with power to provide the best places for children to learn and to help them build powerful brains that are organized and equipped for the challenges in their future.

This think positive and think of the possibilities attitude is seen by teachers throughout the country. A couple of years ago this author wrote,

Education systems and the people who educate youth generally do not understand how students learn. Educators of older students are well advised to know what is going on in the brain as it organizes itself for learning. Perfectly, strategically, systematically designed instructional materials will not work unless they are presented by teachers who are knowledgeable and can make good instructional decisions. Timely and instantaneous decisions must be made during instructional time. These rapid responses are based on how the class is responding to learning at that time and in that place. There are no instructional materials available that can account for and prompt teachers for all the possible scenarios that could occur during each lesson with that particular mix of learners. It takes an accomplished teacher. (Nevills, 2011, p. 103)

A BOLD APPROACH TO LESSON PLANNING

The common core demands instructional shifts that result in a different approach to student learning. For students to learn deeply, to move into more complex subject matter, to interact with information in challenging ways, and to learn to think critically, a new way of planning lessons is needed. In Chapter 2 a variation of commonly used lesson planning was introduced. Here is an even more innovative plan for lesson design. This type of planning is influenced by learning insights from neuroscience and matches the logical, yet curious patterns of the human brain. To redirect how teachers think about instruction, consider these instructional strategies that can be richly rewarding at any level or grade. They brazenly intensify student interest and engagement with attention to lesson stimuli, novelty, associations, task demands, and an appropriate level of difficulty.

Strength of sensory stimulation: Use vivid pictures, colorful labels, soft or loud verbal input, rhythmic chants, and employ students as teachers. These examples change sensory input and create excitement for learning.

Novelty and curiosity: Uncover a secret, give students an unusual set of directions or unusual problems, follow clues, solve puzzles, find missing pieces, and unwrap the talk about a controversial issue to pique students' curiosity.

Associations: Activate background experience and positive feelings for learning success, discover commonalities or differences, build trust relationships, try questioning techniques for personal interest, and expand resources to people, places, or things outside school; each are ways to build associations in the human brain for recall.

Task demands: Plan tasks that are purposeful, beneficial, interesting, sensible, and age-related to appeal to the thought-expanding student mind.

Level of success: Integrate the right level of task difficulty for assignments and projects so students are challenged, feel they can successfully complete the assignment, seek the reward of a job well done, have pride in their work, and attain a new level of understanding.

Lesson plans that demand deep levels of learning are designed by teachers through a new level of planning. Expectations expressed by the common core require teachers themselves to employ cognitive inquiry as they plan for lessons and expanded units of study. Eight questions prompt teachers to think through planning that accepts this serious challenge to engage students at increasingly extended levels.

PLANNING QUESTIONS

1. What do students learn in this unit of study?

To start a lesson topic teachers identify the big learning needs. With the common core, fundamental learning happens in the early grades and builds into complex thinking for the high school years. For a few years there will be a mismatch of what students have been prepared to do and what students are able to do well during their last years of schooling. But that does not mean to wait until children, who are prepared in the new ways of learning and producing, reach high school. Teachers are working now to push hard on the curriculum for expanded results. They are throwing out old ways of teaching and bringing in new dynamic ways of learning. So the first step to plan instruction is to identify exactly what common core outcomes are expected for the students.

Sample Expectations From the Common Core

Learning plans look different depending on the grade level. Primary grade plans are more likely to be focused on single or a small number of precise outcomes. Plan designs for older students reflect integration of content areas and are likely to be less specific. Problems students tackle frequently have more than one successful response. Examples from the common core for the different content areas are given here and can be found at http://www.corestandards.org/resources:

- Writing: The ability to write logical arguments based on substantive claims, sound reasoning, and relevant evidence is a cornerstone of the writing standards, with opinion writing—a basic form of argument—extending down into the earliest grades.
- Speaking and Listening: The standards require that students gain, evaluate, and present increasingly complex information, ideas, and evidence through listening and speaking as well as through media.
- Language: The standards expect that students will grow their vocabularies through a mix of conversations, direct instruction, and reading. The standards will help students determine word meanings, appreciate the nuances of words, and steadily expand their repertoire of words and phrases.
- Mathematics (Primary): The K–5 standards provide students with a *solid foundation in whole numbers, addition, subtraction, multiplication, division, fractions, and decimals*—which help young students build the foundation to successfully apply more demanding math concepts and procedures, and move into applications.
- Mathematics (Secondary): The high school standards call on students to *practice applying mathematical ways of thinking to real world issues and challenges;* they prepare students to think and reason mathematically.
- Science (Sample of Crosscutting Concepts): Patterns: Observed patterns of forms and events guide organization and classification and they prompt questions about relationships and the factors that influence them.

Lessons based on student learning require them to draw on the creativity and integration of thoughts based on their unique life and learning experiences. To get the desired learning outcomes, teachers pose tasks that contain words like *validate, explore, formalize, integrate,* or *defend.* The first step of planning is to look at the big picture to tell what students will be able to do at the end of this learning sequence, and then to break out the smaller learning tasks that are designed to support learning along the way.

Task Analysis

Deciding the smaller tasks, a task analysis, of the skills needed for students to be successful is vitally important. With the common core, the smaller task requirements are designed for the early foundational years, but until the new common core system has had a chance to work its way through the system, it is essential, and will continue to be important, to identify all the initial skills required for a big task. Here is a situation that happened to a very young but highly dedicated student teacher.

> *Madeline was in her second teaching assignment. She was scheduled for an observation of her third-grade class by her university advisor. Her class loved her for her enthusiasm and for the personal care she expressed for each student, and they wanted her to get a good report. Madeline was scheduled to teach a lesson on the dictionary. The students would learn how to use the guide words at the top of each page. This new teacher gave a stellar lesson and covered each of the steps of the university-provided lesson plan. When she came to the guided learning part of the plan she began to question the students and no one was able to answer her questions. They tried, but it was obvious that they were just guessing. She used every teaching tool she could think of, even saying, "Here is what I am thinking as I approach this task . . . " Student frustration was high. Teacher frustration was even more obvious. The lesson abruptly ended as the students were released for recess early.*

This situation has a high potential for reoccurring as the common core expectations for deep, expansive learning come into classrooms. The common core is so much more demanding of students' brain power. Students may not have the foundational skills needed to be successful. In this very elementary example, the children did not know how to alphabetize words, and some may not have mastered the sequence of the alphabet well enough to know letter placement outside of singing the ABC song. If problems occur at elementary levels, imagine the complex task analysis required to teach a unit for an interrelated science class. When all the skills needed for student successful progression are not discovered during initial planning, teachers are required to stop and interject mini lessons to keep students progressing.

A journey into an eighth-grade English/language arts classroom is provided by an experienced teacher. She identified that the students needed to learn how to find and articulate the central ideas or themes of text from a variety of content areas. The English/Language Arts Standards require students to find key ideas and details, to analyze their development, and to summarize the key supporting details. She selected an article about immigrant farmers and read the article aloud. Students read the article on their own. Next the whole class analyzed word choice, structures and features, such as titles, captions, and subheadings, and reexamined the first and last paragraphs. They looked for ideas that were repeated. Their teacher prompted them with questions that were progressively difficult and used terms like *inference.* But the students were not prepared to think in these terms. Mental connections were not in place for them to have information, skills, or concepts that would allow them to respond with understanding (Gewertz, 2013).

This type of experience can be expected in the next few years as students' thinking abilities are challenged at new and higher levels. What do teachers do? They break down the intended big outcome into smaller successes and build on individual skill attainment to reach higher goals. This type of teaching will take more time until students with a strong base in the foundations of learning move through the grades.

> ## 2. What common core subjects and standards are integrated into this lesson?

It is interesting how the common core expectations have been defined for English, Language Arts, Mathematics, and the Next Generation Science Standards. There are expectations and outcomes but no new curriculum, scope and sequence, or tangible materials. The common core standards themselves do provide resource lists of materials that are available online at no cost and some that can be purchased for ELA. While the education system is sorting all this out, the common core is being implemented. Teacher groups are working on scope and sequence, textbook and resource companies are scrambling to decide where they fit into a school system that is looking more heavily into information that is computer accessed, and the assessment people are forging ahead with how this new learning approach will be assessed. It seems that educators would be wise to develop teaching units and learning strategies, test them out, find out what works, and then finalize a scope and sequence process that identifies what resources are lacking. Find what works, then formalize it.

Questions, Questions, and More Questions

With the common core the use of questions as a teaching tool becomes critical. Questions that have previously permeated classrooms, convergent questions, lead to a common set of responses. Questions of this type focus on narrow teaching objectives and prescribed answers. They center student thinking on knowledge and comprehension levels of understanding. With learning outcomes that are reflective of deeper thought, questioning techniques take on new importance. Consider questions that are divergent and elicit a wide range of student responses and in-depth exploration. These big questions are carefully crafted and encourage multiple responses.

Keys to developing a safe environment where students are willing to give responses require teachers to develop these habits.

Resist repeating student responses to encourage students to listen attentively to their peers.

Insist that students speak clearly and loud enough for all to hear.

Accept students' free responses with "no put-down" tactics.

Allow students to speak their complete thoughts without interruptions.

Acknowledge that student responses are important.

Enrich discussions by asking other students to repeat, question, or expand upon a previous student response.

Redirect, as needed, if information is inaccurate, by positively acknowledging the reply, but following with a new question that prompts or redirects. (Orlich, Harder, Callahan, and Gibson, 2001)

Essential questions are defined as the use of provocative questions that interrogate the content. If the teaching content provides the answers, then what are the questions that help students learn? Teachers are encouraged to lead students to well-known content answers, and then to overturn the topic by challenging the answers and deepening understanding (McTighe & Wiggins, 2013). The topic of essential questions is addressed with more depth in the next chapter. What is happening in the human brain when this interrogative type of learning technique is enforced?

Brain Activity

Students learn by drawing on what they already know in long-term memory and working to infuse new ideas. While some of this happens in the working memory area of the brain, the hippocampus, the frontal lobes are called into action for questions that cannot be solved easily. The association areas of the basal ganglia function with the frontal cortex to analyze and coordinate thoughts. The thalamus, deep in the primitive area of the brain also comes into action as it filters information that attempts to intrude into thinking but is unimportant. See Chapter 9 for a diagram of the brain parts consciously and unconsciously involved with the brain's filtering system. When this type of deep thinking is happening, the working areas of the brain are not only activated, but also new connections among neurons are forged and reinforced. Novel, expanded concepts and ideas remain. A smooth route is developed when new pathways are accessed continually. The fresh ideas or extended thoughts are then stored in permanent long-term memory. Students must concentrate and be engaged at excitatory levels for deep learning to occur. It takes rehearsal, practice, and repetitions to cement learning in the brain.

Determining what content areas can be integrated into a lesson and what questions can be used to unpack the content is infinitely exciting. Not only are students' minds expanded with the definition of learning outcomes with the common core, but teachers are also freed to think outside their previous position of teaching specifically what is tested. Now the art of teaching can be unleashed as teachers call on their own thinking brains with new innovative demands.

3. What resources and support are needed to provide the content for this lesson or unit of study?

The possibilities are endless. Work with a peer or the department team. Check teacher teaching teachers' websites and forage into teacher blogs. Think of new ways to provide rote practice and help students master procedural foundations. Decide what information needs to be cemented in nondeclarative memory for instant recall and how that rote type of information can be practiced and maintained for bigger learning.

Gather information online and provide websites for students to access. Prepare a recorded lecture or lesson so students can view or listen to it more than one time. Create a classroom discussion board to work on essential questions outside of classroom time. Talk or collaborate directly with experts in the field from the community or communicate with them virtually. In addition to using the textbook, include other primary and secondary source materials or documents. Select books that students can read with an e-reader allowing them to mark text and make comments. All this planning takes time. And time well spent it is. As teachers become more involved with creating new ways for students to learn, they become animated and eager to share these new ways of doing school with their students.

4. How long will it take to complete this learning unit?

In the primary grades, the foundations for more complex learning are being developed. Although primary grade expectations are changed from the previous standards, the time for lessons and units of study remains relatively unchanged. Integrated, expanded units and projects appear in the middle and upper elementary years, and are fully integrated into the curriculum of the secondary grades. Learning at deeper levels demands more time and topics. See Table 3.1 in Chapter 3 for a comparison of the previous standards and the CCSS.

Think big. Think of big projects, big questions, deep learning, and global implications. Build in more classroom time by identifying and starting with the fundamentals and advancing to big thinking projects. One of the many advantages of the CCSS is that it relieves teachers from the burden of covering so much material with little depth. The requirements allow the luxury of time for learning that is expansive and covers an array of content. What students learn is at a level of intensity for long-term memory and remembering.

5. What lesson design tools and input resources are needed?

There are many stimulating resources and teaching strategies for teachers to consider that vitally support student learning. Previously designed lessons can morph into blended learning, discovery or inquiry, a flipped classroom approach, a series of mini lectures, or many other creative teach-to-learn approaches. Add to these various media, reading devices, and ways of electronic communication and the world opens to every classroom.

Teachers are able to find the best counterparts to any learning experience, while they match resources to outcomes. It is not effective to adopt a flipped lesson design for use every day, for example. This currently popular strategy, where students view a lecture or talk outside the classroom and have interaction about the lesson with the teacher, is one creative approach to maximizing classroom time. Sometimes the process for a flipped learning project is the best way for information or a process to be presented. When used prudently, it is novel and creates learning excitement. If the flipped classroom approach is continually used, it becomes monotonous and routine and loses its initial appeal. Basically, while students' brains like the comfort of routine, they seek uniqueness to be stimulated and become attentive to new information. Matching the resources to the desired learning output in different ways for each big unit maintains teacher and student enthusiasm for learning.

In a first-grade classroom, for example, the students are expected to describe the connections between two individuals, events, ideas, or pieces of information in a text. It is important to know that the students know and can apply the academic language for the words, connections, individuals, and ideas (literacy 1.3). One way to accomplish this outcome is to give a piece of yarn about five feet long to one-third of the children. They are asked to find two children without yarn and ask each hold an end of the yarn. The child with the yarn and the two others form a group of three. The small group is asked to figure out something besides the yarn that connects the two children holding the yarn. The team may discover that "they both have brown eyes" or "they are wearing tennis shoes," for example. With this simple activity children would learn and likely remember the meaning of connection, individuals, and ideas that could then be applied to their text.

In a tenth- or eleventh-grade chemistry lab an example standard is HS-PS1–2: Construct and revise an explanation for the outcome of a simple chemical reaction based on the outermost electron states of atoms, trends in the periodic table, and knowledge of the patterns of chemical properties. Student activities of predicting, observing, and explaining following an experiment with a simple chemical alteration is merely the beginning of the task for this standard. The initial response may be a right answer, but it is not a preferred answer. In this case, the students' teacher asks essential questions, probes for more details, and directs students to gather information about the electron states of an atom and how the new information impacts the reaction they witnessed. The periodic table is scrutinized while students seek a deeper understanding for patterns among chemical properties. The beginning student response is revised and revised again, until the product represents the best thinking of each individual or of the group. Interestingly, the final answers may be brought up again at a later time or in a higher grade level for more depth of understanding.

> **6. How can students be most actively engaged for learning? What does the classroom need to look like?**

There are many ways to structure student configurations for learning tasks.

- Work individually.
- Start work individually, and then at a specified time be joined by others.
- Work with a partner.
- Be assigned to a small group.
- Begin with a small group, and then join another group.
- Begin with a small group, and then work to complete an individual task.
- Work individually or in a group, and then come together to complete a whole class project.

Teachers are encouraged to keep in mind the term *agile learning spaces.* The image of a classroom does not need to reflect the typical classroom with rows of desks. The size of the classroom, number of students, and size of the students may encourage or limit flexibility. One sixth-grade teacher wanted a flexible classroom but had over 30 students, big desks to accommodate the students, and a classroom that would be just fine for students the size of third graders. The solution was to move learning groups to the outside picnic tables that were within vision of the classroom windows. Certainly this is not a possible response for all teachers; however, it is a creative response to an inherent problem. Other solutions may be to occasionally move to the cafeteria or schedule another unused area depending on the school building. Teachers think about pushing outside the concrete walls of the classroom by going into the community to schedule a class period, or extending the classroom by inviting online peers to join a lesson. One community, the Green River educational Cooperative in Kentucky serves a large sparsely populated area. When the cooperative was awarded Race to the Top grant funding, it was decided to use the money for a glaring problem. Many of the students did not have access to the Internet at home. They were spending large amounts of time daily traveling to and from school. The solution was to spend grant money to put WI-FI on school buses, where students do school work and investigative study while they travel (McNeil, 2013).

The elements of classrooms for active learning are diverse. Here are some materials and setup ideas:

- Computer, projector, screen, white board, smart boards, bulletin boards, or chalk board
- Chart rack/s, lots of paper, and wall space for hanging
- Student-developed class standards (selected from a teacher provided list)
- Space for movement, project development, and project display
- Notebooks and journals
- Progress chart/s for student and teacher evaluation systems
- Student incentive system (external and/or internal)
- Plentiful resources, hard copy, online, community based
- Internet access
- Instructional use of cell phones, tablets, and laptops

7. What intermittent and ongoing teacher support is needed for students to progress with their work?

Students work must be more learning directed to meet the common core standards. Teachers spend less time in front of the classroom teaching. With new learning expectations students more frequently work in groups. Teachers become a part of student groups, ask essential or thought provoking questions, and provide new information or resources. Intermittently, teachers call the class together to model a way of thinking, clarify product development, or to teach a mini lesson on a concept that students are missing. Similarly the class may come together to check for understanding or for group or individual reports of progress. Teachers provide constant evaluation, give feedback on progress, and provide opportunities for individuals or groups to exhibit their learning progress. In an active learning classroom, this could mean charts on the wall, a table for displays, a bulletin board, a PowerPoint show, an active classroom blog, discussion board, or wiki post. By using these interactive processes, teachers offer a way for students to give feedback or suggest resources for each other.

8. How will students show the progression of their learning?

The possibilities seem endless, but a brainstormed list of possibilities includes the following:

- Research a topic and write and present a report.
- Do a project that expands and demonstrates learning.
- Tackle essential, big questions that develop over the course of the school year.
- Write a persuasive essay that begs for readers to form a new perspective.
- Make a presentation that uses at least one form of technology.
- Provide pros and cons of a current controversial issue.
- Teach others to find and strengthen a new concept.
- Show competency through problem solving.
- Rewrite a chapter or outcome of an assigned reading.
- Make a prediction at the onset of the learning and revisit it at a later time.
- Integrate new information into a new way of expression.
- Develop a test for others to take and plan how it will be scored and discussed.
- Take part in a debate. Halfway through the exercise, change to defend the other side of the issue.
- Justify a thinking outcome with facts and evidence.
- Interpret for another student, for whom the information is new.
- Defend or rethink an opinion by interviewing people in the field.
- Critique and provide feedback on another student's work.
- Appraise the reliability of one or more resources.

- Illustrate a new concept by making a drawing, cartoon, or poster.
- Self-evaluate depth of learning using a scale 1, 2, or 3 (1—development of an awareness, 2—know enough to talk about it, 3—know it well enough to teach others).
- Design a product to learn and demonstrate something newly discovered.

This method of teaching looks like teachers leading and students learning. New attitudes emerge with a wave of creative possibilities. Kelly Marcy from Iredell-Statesville district in North Carolina addressed this change.

There is less lecture, less students sitting in [*sic*] desk. There will be more of a rotation around project-based learning and small-group instruction, and more work happening on a device. More subtle will be that the teacher is the leader. (McNeil, 2013)

So Many Ways to Learn: What Students Do

Students can be fired up about learning; it is a brain thing. When they understand how the three pound mass of neural cells works, they are able to take charge of their own learning. This chapter provides unique information using the format from the book Build the Brain for Reading, Grades 4–12 *(Nevills, 2011). Students are invited to understand the human brain and how it works consciously and unconsciously for their benefit. It is an extension of the previous chapter that focuses on how teachers plan for explosive learning at all grade levels. This one provides strategies to enrich the core standards and develop students who love to learn.*

Teachers can talk with their students about the important role they play in this new drama of common core learning under the same system called education. Rather than students coming to school to find out what the teacher has planned for them, they are being asked to know and own the huge responsibility of higher order and cognitively challenging learning.

School can be an exciting place as students grow to understand their own cognitive abilities and gain appreciation of the brain that allows them to do amazing feats. They also become aware of the strategies that are effective for different learning challenges. To help learners gain awareness of the brain they possess, teachers can provide brain bits of information that become an owner's manual of sorts.

Teachers are invited to share information with their students in the book, *Build the Brain for Reading, Grades 4–12* by this author (2011). The book explains how students build on the foundation of decoding and fluent reading in the early grades to build skills for comprehension and understanding during reading in fourth grade and beyond. To do this feat, teachers learn and share with their students what stimulates the different parts of the learner's brain to make connections and to draw on prior experiences to make new ones. It is an awesome process as the brain forms networks of connections, strengthens them, and is able to recall at will information that has been read.

In many ways, it is more difficult to become competent at learning from reading text than it is to learn the stages needed to read that text. *Learning to read* in the early grades is prescriptive and follows a direct instructional sequence. *Reading to learn* in the upper grades follows a challenging, diverse, often undetermined route. The same format used in the previously mentioned book is provided here. The narratives given can be read to or by students. Teachers are encouraged to provide additional information and to develop critical questions that draw information from the students for a deeper depth of understanding themselves as learners.

WHAT COULD YOU DISCUSS WITH YOUR STUDENTS ABOUT HOW THEY USE THEIR BRAINS FOR REMEMBERING?

It is important to understand your brain as the thinking organ in your body that receives input from the senses. Without information from the five senses, the mind would have nothing to think about. The work horses of the brain are miniscule nerve cells called neurons. Your neurons become active to make neural highways that connect useful thoughts. When you think real hard about something and keep rehearsing or practicing there is a better chance you will remember the information. With some basic brain information, young and older learners can identify how they work to remember and how they learn best. Some want to learn by seeing words, pictures, or viewing a video, while others want to be actively engaged with the information by talking, writing, or drawing. Some students like to make their own sketches, diagrams, or charts. Each student uses different practices for the variety of things they are attempting to remember. What works best for you?

Figure 6.1 Sample Classroom Poster for Student Engagement

1. Students learn when they listen to or watch someone else who is modeling.

2. Students learn

powerfully when they engage in the action of learning.

BUILD IN BRAIN PRACTICES

To start, here are some ways learners can experience and force their brains to respond. The first is an activity to experience what it feels like to concentrate. Identify first the difference between *paying attention* and *concentrating*. Anyone can pay attention by looking at the person; at school, students usually are attending to the teacher, who is talking. But, while appearing to pay attention, the student can be actually thinking about and concentrating on something else—a bad hair day, who said what to whom, wanting to check social media to find out what is happening with friends, and so on. But concentrating on the subject for a class requires deeper levels of conscious thought.

Experience Concentrating

Here is an activity to use with learners.

1. Select a relatively simple, convergent question that has many more answers than one. For example, "Name four of the most recent presidents of the United States." Or "If you had a hundred dollars to spend, name four things you could buy." Choose a number of responses that is appropriate for the level of your students, for example, three for third graders and as many as five for high school students.

2. Have students work with a partner.

3. Tell the students you will ask them a question everyone can answer. When you say, "Go" they will think of the answers **but not say them or write them**. They will have ample time to think of their answers. They will be telling their answers with their partners only when you say, "Share your answers."

4. Give the question and say, "Go."

5.   Wait an extra ordinate amount of time, maybe as long as a minute, depending on the age of the students. Then give the prompt tó share their answers.

6.   After the students have given their answers, ask them to tell how they felt and what they thought during the time they waited to talk. Work with questions that challenge their feelings and deepen their understanding of what happened during this short exercise. Repeat this experience intermittently to support students as they learn knowledge level lists.

This is what it feels like to consciously force the human brain to concentrate. This is the hard work of learning, particularly learning under the common core. Learners must concentrate on what they want to learn by holding the information in their working memory. Exercising the hippocampus like this happens by practicing, associating, and rehearsing. When students hold information in working memory for a sufficient amount of time, which may take intermittent practice, the human brain is designed to take that important information and store it with other information that is similar. It may be stored as a visual memory, for its auditory features, in the deep emotional center, and in the frontal area of the brain for its concepts and higher level thought. This second part of the remembering process transpires unconsciously and depends on each student's unique connective brain structures. Students can be prompted to concentrate by brainy words, such as **Fire Up**, **Connect**, **Activate**, or **Focus**!

The Brain—A Pattern-Seeking Organ

Patterns, logic, rhythms, assortments, and order through lists all appeal to the human brain. Unconsciously, the brain is designed to sort through vast amounts of information in an attempt to find a place to best file it—if it is important. While the brain's sensory memory system drops out most of the signals from the environment that it receives, some information finds its way to working memory for consideration. Input that is important to the individual is retained for thought and possibly for deep concentration. And the brain must decide on its own, without conscious effort from the owner, just where it will be stored for long term. So it makes perfect sense that if information is provided in a logical, orderly manner, it is easier for the brain to unconsciously sort and store information with other similar material. Systematic thinking is perfect for the frameworks and standards that pervaded the education system previously, but it is merely a start for the common core.

Students learn patterns for the foundational skills, which eventually lead to deeper thinking. And there are many ways to reinforce building a strong brain framework for forever learning. What learning activities support the pattern seeking brain?

Any time the activity involves organizing, sorting, comparing, listing, or finding similarities or differences, a child's brain builds a good foundation for remembering. These activities permeate classroom and particularly workbook assignments. And they have a purpose, as long as it is known that learning is at the knowledge and comprehension, or possibly the application levels. These activities can continue for foundational skills, but they are not going to be adequate for the deep learning demanded from the common core.

Rhyming, Rhythms, and Chants

In the very early grades everyone acknowledges the importance of the order of the alphabet. It is learned by singing the letters to the tune of "Twinkle, Twinkle Little Star." Children learn their phone numbers and addresses easily when they are chanted in a sing song pattern. Older students often learn math facts through a jingle or rap rhythm. Science teachers turn to song to engage students in concepts that need to have rapid recall. Clapping is frequently added or hand movements. Innovative teachers have students stand and move to reinforce learning that needs to be at the automatic level.

Thinking Maps

There are a variety of visual aids to prompt thinking that is both at the foundational and deeper levels. They include having students develop diagrams, tables, figures, and timelines; translation of a technical writing into everyday language; questioning and answering; and Thinking Maps.

Some work with graphic organizers and mind mapping as learning activities ran their course. Actually the format became more of a teacher activity, because teachers labored to develop structures for students to fill in. It was more of a teacher requirement than a student learning task. That is until David Hyerle showed teachers a new way to challenge student thinking. Hyerle, along with his colleagues, selected the term *Thinking Maps* to more closely align with the serious work the human mind is capable of achieving. Thinking Maps as visual aids have five qualities: (1) consistence, (2) flexibility, (3) development, (4) integration, and (5) reflection. All these dynamic qualities work to embrace the common core standards. Students select from a variety of formats, which comprise of the traditional circle or bubble, and also include a tree or bridge map. See Figure 6.2 for a variety of computer generated shapes that can be introduced. Students' developing work is reflective of the five qualities.

1. Consistence—the map format selected and the symbols used remain relatively the same throughout the process of map development.

2. Flexibility—the map grows uniquely and incrementally with information and details of the selected topic.

3. Development—the overall shape and map design continue to emerge with various connections.

4. Integration—during map construction a new thought process may develop and need to be expressed by bridging to a new format.

5. Reflection—the final product is wrapped in a rectangular box and ready for consideration by study partners, a process group, or as an assessment tool.

Figure 6.2   Computer Shapes That Can Be Used for Thinking Maps

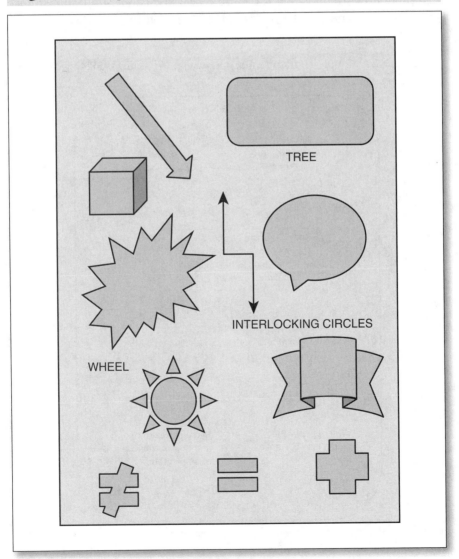

To move beyond the basic formats of the circle, bubble, bridge, or tree, teachers can use hand drawn shapes or access the SmartArt tab available in Microsoft Word. Teachers can select a variety of shapes for students to use with the five qualities that are listed.

Teachers introduce Thinking Maps or other visual aids by telling what they are thinking and by modeling a visual aid design. The most powerful learning, the type of learning required in the common core, happens when students work on their own to determine the structure or format they need to show information from their own unique memory systems (Hyerle, Alper, & Curtis, 2004).

Expanded Questioning

There are questions and there are questions. The best questions make students think and give them enough time to reflect on their answers or

Figure 6.3 Sample Thinking Map With Computer Generated Shapes

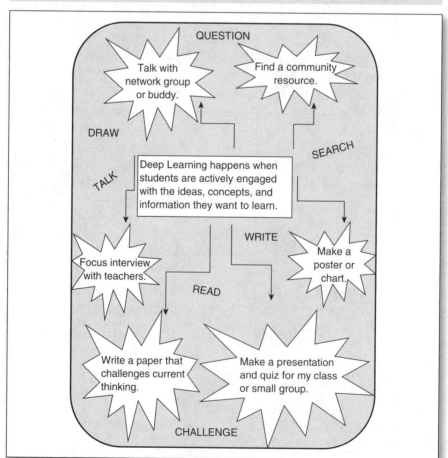

those of their peers. Some teachers are inherently gifted at posing questions that dig deeply into the content. Their questions do not let students "off the hook" with the initial blush of an answer. Other teachers may need to plan ahead for questions they think will stimulate the extensive discussion needed for the topic. As mentioned earlier, it is often difficult to predict the direction student thinking may go, and learning outcomes can have surprising results.

Classrooms that are humming with activity, with standards in place for honoring all students and their contributions, and have a teacher, as a creative leader, can move student learning to unimagined depths. A word of caution is needed. In a trust environment, it is important for teachers to refrain from using essential questions to give their own personal views or preferences. The preferences of students and teachers alike are best when they are supported by facts and valid evidence. McTighe and Wiggins (2013) address care and nurturing classroom rules to effectively use essential questions. Some suggestions are provided (see Table 6.1).

Leading and Guiding Questions

Prior to employing essential questions there are questions for leading and guiding students' thinking. *Leading questions* are rhetorical questions that have correct answers. They are used initially to prompt the brain to locate information that will be needed for more challenging work. *Guiding questions* are not truly open ended, either. Instead they require some explanation and support. Their purpose is to guide students to knowledge and

Table 6.1   Essential Questions Become a Dynamic Classroom Learning Experience When Some Classroom Rules Are Posted or Understood Inherently

Classroom Agreement for Question and Answer Activities
1. Questions often have many different answers, just like life has many possibilities.
2. Important ideas are developed over time.
3. Some questions are ongoing and will be posted in the class.
4. Everyone in this class is a participant by listening and responding.
5. The strength of any idea can be challenged and tested without meaning that the response or the person is not valued.
6. Answers can be questioned.
7. Mistaken answers happen and are acknowledged as a part of learning.

information that has previously been learned and stored in association areas of the brain. Thoughts resulting from these two types of questions are gathered into the students' conscious working memory where they can be fused with new ideas.

McTighe and Wiggins (2013) provide convincing examples of how *essential questions* can be a vital part of learning. Questioning activities not only lead to answers in content areas, but also overturn the topics by challenging answers that are correct but beg for deeper understanding. At times these questions position students to move outside the classroom and look for answers to questions that have not been solved.

Here are examples for the primary grades:

- How can our class help people who are homeless in the community?
- What do third graders need to know about the police in our city?
- What is the hardest book you have read? Tell why it was hard to read and what you did to overcome the difficulty.
- What could this class do to make the principal's job easier?
- What do parents need to know about our class?

Examples for secondary grades are these:

- What would it take for us to use the ocean as a source of drinking water?
- Are there alternative fuels for cars that should replace our reliance on fossil fuel?
- How could a classroom blog be used to expand our learning outside the classroom?
- What are some problems in this community, and who would we talk to, to find out what we could do to help?
- After reading an article in a current magazine or journal, what would you put in a letter to the editor?
- If another member of your family were to be in this class, what would they need to know to be successful?

Overarching essential questions, the big questions, have answers that are appropriate to visit over and over again across the grades and across the curriculum. "What are the rules for mathematics that are useful?" and "What causes people to move from one location to another (social studies)?" Essential questions can be developed for every area of the curriculum and can continue to stimulate discussion across grade levels, which is exactly what is requested in the common core.

Self Monitoring and Metacognition

To accomplish common core expectations, teachers cannot carry the heavy burden of student learning. Students must carry that load, and being able to self monitor is a big part of that responsibility. Students are encouraged to be in charge of their own outcomes for learning when they understand the miraculous feats of their brain. And equally important is their ability to intervene and control the action. Here are some of the questions that prompt students to be prepared to as learners (see Table 6.2).

Table 6.2 Self Monitoring Is a Way to Help Students Be Responsible for Learning

Self Monitoring Questions for Students
Am I satisfied with my performance? If not what can I do to improve it?
What am I learning? What new insights have I found?
What is working for me right now? How might I adjust or redirect?
What is my backup plan if I get stuck?
Am I being effective with the time I have for this task?
Do I need some feedback on this project? Who will talk this over with me?

Stopping every once in a while to reflect on studying or the job at hand is a helpful habit. Students can be given a list of questions, such as this one or one important monitoring question, and be prompted to stop at intervals to reflect on their progress. Realize that every learning situation is not going to be the ideal stimulation for every student. But responsible learners need to stay on target. It is helpful to talk this situation over with students.

HOW CAN YOU HELP YOUR STUDENTS TAKE THE CHALLENGE THE COMMON CORE DEMANDS?

Sometimes we learn just enough to get by. Then that topic comes up again, and we realize how sketchy our learning actually was and that we have to go back and build the basics for that topic. When a new unit or topic is introduced students are fortunate if it is presented in a way that is interesting, novel, challenging, yet possible to be completed successfully. What

(Continued)

(Continued)

new units or subjects can you think of that appealed to you because of the way they were introduced and what appealed to you about the work you were asked to do?

At other times it is "school as usual" and there is nothing to grab your attention, but you still have to do the assignment and learn the process or information. What can you do to make each new school challenge meaningful and possible? Some suggestions may be to challenge yourself to earn a couple more points on the assignment, or to maintain a previous level of success, to promise yourself a reward at the end of the task, or to keep a chart of what you need to do and get the satisfaction of checking it off when it is complete. The idea here is for you to do self monitoring and not expect someone else to prompt and remind you.

Use essential questions to help students realize what skills they already have perfected and identify those that need to be encouraged. Arming students with information about who they are as learners helps them reflect about what they are doing and examine why it is important for them to be engaged with school.

A Study and Practice Episode

Helping students know how much practice and rehearsal they need is an important task. A study by Willingham (2009) with a group of young adults found what the researcher termed as a "not studying enough" dilemma. By asking a series of questions about general domain knowledge, he discovered that students may be more confident about their level of learning than they actually are. His process can be replicated in the classroom.

1. Select questions from your content area that are not too easy or too hard. These are questions that most students would be challenged a bit to answer. For example:

   Can you give the names of at least six of the characters from Star Wars?

   Or, can you name the states that are located on the eastern seaboard of the United States?

   Teachers may wish to use questions from units of study completed earlier in the school year. The question requires a "yes" or "no" answer written on a paper with the questions. Students answer "yes" if they can supply the answer or "no" if they cannot.

2. Next, the students are given another paper with the questions and asked to respond to the questions by writing their answers.

3. Students self-check to see which answers are complete and accurate. Then the class examines how accurate the students were at determining whether or not they knew the answer.

If the students are similar to the ones tested by Willingham, it is likely the students think they know answers, while they actually cannot perform at their anticipated level and with the accuracy the questions demand. The researcher concludes that students generally need to spend 20% more time studying than they anticipate. The extra amount of time secures information into long-term memory for instant, accurate, and complete recall. Students come up with their own conclusions about their level of learning and need for study as a result of this experience.

WHAT CAN YOU DISCUSS WITH YOUR STUDENTS ABOUT OVERCONFIDENCE AND WHAT THEY NEED TO DO TO DEVELOP DEEP LEVELS OF LEARNING?

To compensate for what you think you know for actual assessments and what you really need to know well, the researcher, Willingham, gave the students a solution. He told them they need to spend about 20% more time studying than they think they need. For example, if you think you need 2 hours to study for an exam and you add 20%, then you need to have 2 hours and 40 minutes available for studying. If you use his suggestion, you will find that during the extra time you will practice, repeat, and connect new ideas. Then you will be more likely to have a deep understanding of the topic, and hopefully your test grades will reflect your extra work and you will have a stronger ability to remember the content. Think also about extending study times over many study periods. Know that you need to activate the remembering pathways in your brain many times for information to be stored in long-term memory.

Students can be prompted by phrases, such as **Practice, Practice, Practice** or **Not Long in the Works** (working memory), **but Forever in Mind** (long-term memory), or **The Hippocampus Rocks!** Understanding individually unique memory systems used for learning is helpful to students so they can pace themselves. It is important not to get overconfident when they learn quicker than others or discouraged when they take more time to study.

Figure 6.4 Sample Classroom Poster for Active Learning

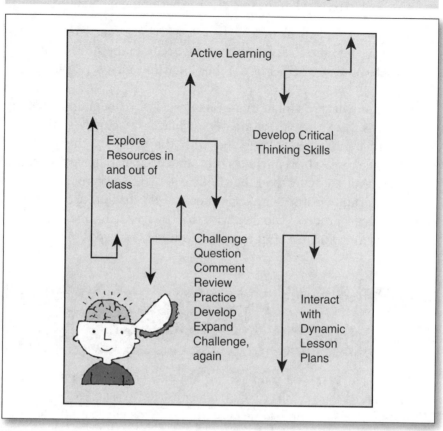

Thinking With the Brain's CEO

Neuroscientists refer to the frontal lobes located at the forehead and extending slightly more than halfway to the back of the head as the brain's chief executive officer, the CEO. This active area of the brain is specifically for executive function (EF). The type of learning and remembering required in the common core requires a different level of brain involvement—more intense. If students, who are intensely involved in a project that answers one of the curriculum's big questions, were placed in a brain scanner, the results would be spectacular to watch. If, for example, the scanning device was for functional magnetic resonance imaging (fMRI), there would be a visual movie-like display. The neurons responsible for the thinking processes cause neurons in the pathway of the connecting thoughts to fire. Firing neurons requires energy. In this case, there is a demand for more blood to the regions involved with thinking. The oxygen in the blood changes the magnetic field. The fMRI scanner picks up the changes and produces detailed, continually changing images on a computer screen.

Viewing a Positron Emission Tomography (PET) scan is equally exciting. PET scans are more cautiously used, because they require an injection of radioactive glucose. So while it is unlikely to happen for students in elementary or secondary school, when it is used, the PET display is viewed in color. The areas of the brain that are less active are seen as blue, purple, or green. Areas that are active have more blood, thus have water molecules. The molecules respond to radio waves that are fired into the brain by the scanner. Colors from the active part of the brain are yellow for moderate activity and red or white for intense thought. Viewing a PET image of a student involved with some heavy thinking would show lots of activity in the right and left frontal lobes and other association areas that are supporting the wave of thinking.

The prefrontal lobes are directly before the sensory and motor areas of the brain and are the structures that make humans unique from other animals. Humans think, remember, problem solve, AND engage in conceptualizing, integrating, product development, and long-term predicting. It is mainly in this area of the brain that execution of long-term planning, self-regulation, sustained mental productivity, and segmentation of space and material occur. This is the pretty heady area of the brain that is tapped to carry out the rigorous demands of the common core standards.

WHAT CONVERSATION COULD TEACHERS HAVE WITH STUDENTS ABOUT NEURONS AND LEARNING?

When you think real hard about something you want to learn, you activate and excite neurons into an unstable state. They are charged up. This charged state makes the axon, an extended tail on each neuron excited to the point that it shivers and sends a chemical out one of its shipping docks. If you are heavy into thinking and concentrating, you most likely are causing a lot of this excitement in the prefrontal area of your brain. It is the area just above your eyes, behind your forehead where intense executive thought occurs. Do you ever catch yourself with your hands over this area, when you are deep in concentration?

The whopping strong chemical movement is fast and intense. As hundreds, thousands, or tens of thousands of other neurons with their multitude of dendrites pick up on the chemicals dumped into the synapse, they too get involved with the thought and shiver an electrical shock from their nucleus. And you know what happens next, the axon spews more chemicals

(Continued)

(Continued)

and more neurons are invited to join that thought, possibly from remote areas of the brain. These dynamic, neuron-stimulating thoughts you are likely to remember.

Conversely, if you half-consciously approach the task and really do not spend much energy concentrating, the neuron signals are weak, actually wimpy. The thought patterns will fade away like you never entertained them. So when you want to remember something and work with it again, you need to expend the energy to think deeply. You may decide to write, draw, talk, question, practice aloud, or quiz yourself to keep the action going. In that way your important brain work will be retained, ready to activate when you are.

As previously presented, teachers have an opportunity to question students about their involvement with learning. Students can enter into metacognitive thinking as they challenge themselves to engage in deep thinking practices. Students may respond to phrases such as **Rehearse, Record, and Remember** or **Stop, Focus, and Attend**. They also like the idea of a **Brain Break.**

Students can be prompted to know when they need a break from cognitive work. Just like muscles of the body, the nerve cells in the brain can become fatigued. They fire and connect so vigorously that they simply need to be refueled. Taking time away from tasks allows the busy areas of the brain to quiet down, and for thinking and learning to solidify. During school or while doing homework, breaks are beneficial. It is best, however, to have a predetermined amount of time for a break, because it can require difficult discipline to get back into brain tasks.

Developing Critical Thinkers

Students are not automatically critical, evaluative thinkers. Patterns of thoughts for discernment and other higher levels of thinking demand development of executive function in the frontal lobes. And higher levels of thinking can begin in the elementary years. Here are some activities with varying levels of difficulty. Some of them have been adapted from John Chaffee's (2009) book *Thinking Critically*, which is a resource that should be available to teachers as they prepare students for the challenges of thinking using the common core expectations. Other examples come from a variety of classrooms throughout the United States.

1. Learn to identify detail, predict, and appreciate differing perspectives.

   Choose a stimulating picture that is appropriate for the age of the students. Ask students to write or tell (and have recorded) what is happening in the picture. Then ask what will happen next. Again, the students write or tell and could also draw a picture. Ask the students what details from the picture lead them to make their predictions. Listen to and list the details, or see pictures from different students. Have students record perceptions their classmates give that differ from theirs.

2. Identify different perspectives and investigative cause.

   Have a person act out a story or scenario (see examples from Reading anchor standard 3 given below), which are related to a unit of study. This person can be a volunteer adult, another teacher, or student from an older grade that students do not know. After the short drama, ask students to make a drawing and write a description of the character and the information presented. Share perceptions and then ask students to respond to these questions: "Why do people describe the character in different or contrasting ways?" and "Why do some children hear, see, and record what was seen differently?"

   The reading language arts standards express that students need to be exposed to "classic myths and stories from around the world, foundational U.S. documents, seminal works of American literature, and the writings of Shakespeare" (Reading anchor standard 3). Furthermore, they are required to be able to show adequate performance levels in writing arguments, informational/explanatory texts, and narratives (Writing anchor standard 3).

3. Determine which speaks louder, a picture or words.

   Choose a paragraph or more from a book students are using that has an accompanying picture. Copy text for half of the class and make the picture available for the other students. Students review their paper, and then pair up with a student who has the other input. **Text and pictures are not shared**. The person with the picture is first to describe what is seen in the picture. Then the person with text summarizes, not reads, the information in no more than four or five sentences. Questions can be asked, as needed, between the pair. Students swap papers to see what was given to their partner.

Call the class together to answer these questions:

- What speaks louder, pictures or words? Take a hand vote.
- Which partner had more accurate information?
- What influenced your decision?
- What might you tell an author or publisher about the use of pictures in a text book?

These examples are used to help students develop critical thought processes. As teachers continue to focus on deeper learning for the common core, many other experiences can be adjusted to direct teachers and students to understand practices that develop critical thinking skills.

Critical Thinking Skill Development Through Metacognition

The term *critical thinking* is vital to the descriptors and the expectations throughout the CCSS. Teachers can use metacognition to teach what students need to develop critical thinking skills. Table 6.3 is provided for this lesson example.

Table 6.3   Characteristics of Expert Critical Thinkers

Give Examples for Each of These Critical Thinking Skills
Open-minded students listen carefully and evaluate fairly.
Knowledgeable thinkers offer opinions based on facts and are honest if they need more information.
Mentally active people consciously confront challenges and problems.
Curious thinkers explore new situations to get to the depth of issues.
Independent thinkers are not afraid to have opinions that differ from the group.
Skilled debaters can give ideas in an orderly and reasonable manner.
Insightful students can move beyond information that is obvious.
Self-aware students know their biases and can speak about them.
Creative thinkers can imagine beyond what already has been discovered and produce new responses.
Passionate learners look at common understandings and issues and seek more clarity.

Source: Modified from Chaffee, 2009, p. 44.

Ask students to think of a time they were startled by their own response or that of a peer because it was right on target, truly an expression of wisdom. Think of this time that you were able to express yourself with a depth of knowledge and logic that you did not think you were capable of expressing. To understand the skills necessary to think at this critical level, John Chaffee (2009) developed a list of characteristics young or older people show when they act in cognitively deep, analytical ways.

1. Provide a copy of the table for each student that has enough room between each characteristic for student writing.

2. Look at the first descriptive statement: *Open-minded students* listen carefully and evaluate fairly. Ask for an example of being open-minded. Be prepared to give a response, if students are not able. An example is "Remember when John listened to his group talk about the importance of having girls on the soccer team and changed his mind?" Then encourage them to add others. Students are expected to record two examples of each characteristic. Step 2 may develop over an extended period of time.

3. Students put a check mark next to each characteristic they have developed, and they highlight at least two others they would like to be able to do.

4. In small groups students seek verification from their peers of the ones checked as developed. Do peers agree with their assessment of their personal critical thinking skills? Finally, students identify the ones that they will select to target for development. Their classmates encourage them with suggestions on how that might happen.

Teachers and students are strongly encouraged to return to this list at regular intervals, and to talk about progress students are making as critical thinkers. Students can identify examples of when they responded or showed behaviors of the skills they selected to develop. Placing this list in a plastic sleeve or posting it in some prominent place helps students realize how important these traits can be.

Use of Media and Technology

The common core expects students to own skills related to media and the use of technology for critical analysis and production of media that is incorporated throughout the curriculum. Teachers are already on to this expectation. Blogging for students taps into their creative thinking as they design a blog that will appeal to the online audience. With the high appeal of global media, students are encouraged to write persuasive, informational, and narrative pieces. There are kid blogs for those who are under

13 years and Gmail or Blogger accounts are available for older students. Student accounts can be created with a site called *Wikispaces*. They can develop their own web pages and integrate images, videos, text, and other plug-ins. Additionally, these cloud-type resources allow students to develop electronic portfolios for digital projects. The common core requires big ideas to carry forward from year to year. Students can draw on an earlier year's digital work to expand beyond what previously had been learned but was not the final answer. Use of technology not only is a way for students to express higher order thinking, but also aligns with the common core.

WHAT CAN STUDENTS UNDERSTAND ABOUT THEIR ROLE AS RESPONSIBLE LEARNERS?

We are all in this school thing together. It is the best place for us to be as a teacher and a class full of learners. To become a teacher, I completed extensive coursework to earn a credential that allows me to have a job as a professional who teaches. Students inherently have a lot to learn. A school environment can be exciting, pertinent, and engaging. Classrooms can be thought of as active laboratories of learners. While I expect my students to focus, concentrate on, interact with, challenge, and practice important concepts from the curriculum, you have expectations of me, as well. Students can expect their teachers to make learning meaningful and engaging, and to set a success level that is attainable by every learner. All learners need to feel safe to try out new ideas and we listen attentively to each other. We need to work together to set up classroom spaces to allow movement and activities. We need to agree on a set of classroom rules or expectancies that prompt us to work effectively. Together, students and teacher, we need to work to maximize our time, to complete the course, and for everyone to enjoy and experience successful learning outcomes.

One Last Useful Idea

This chapter has a fun, almost whimsical feeling to some very serious learning activities. Learning can be enjoyable. In addition to a myriad of learning activities, discussion points for learning about learning are provided. One last thought is to print out sayings about education from notable sources to explore and post in your classroom. Consider these that were found at http://www.brainyquote.com

If you can't explain it simply, you don't understand it well enough.

—Albert Einstein

It's not that I'm so smart, it's just that I stay with problems longer.

—Albert Einstein

Education is what remains after one has forgotten what one has learned in school.

—Albert Einstein

The only thing that interferes with my learning is my education.

—Albert Einstein

It is the mark of an educated mind to be able to entertain a thought without accepting it.

—Aristotle

An education isn't how much you have committed to memory, or even how much you know. It's being able to differentiate between what you know and what you don't.

—Anatole France

Education is an admirable thing, but it is well to remember from time to time that nothing that is worth knowing can be taught.

—Oscar Wilde

Education is not the filling of a pail, but the lighting of a fire.

—William Butler Yeats

Finally,

No one has yet realized the wealth of sympathy, the kindness and generosity hidden in the soul of a child. The effort of every true education should be to unlock that treasure.

—Emma Goldman

Powerful Staff Development for Adult Learners

Professional development can be different to respond to the common core by moving beyond what has always been done. Understanding adult learners helps shed light on how teachers can learn most expeditiously what has not been learned before. By understanding themselves as learners, teachers feel what their students need to do to learn, regardless of their grade level. The focus here is on teachers as learners, teachers as leaders among their peers, teachers as leaders for student learning, and teachers challenged to think, plan, and learn together like they have never done before.

What can be different about staff development with the common core? What new skills are teachers asked to develop? Districts are grappling with the problem of how to do professional development for the common core because it demands more than has been demanded previously. Teachers need retooling, rethinking, smarter planning, and different delivery of instruction. Teacher "buy in" is particularly important. Only through collaboration can this dramatic change be navigated for a successful transition.

STAFF DEVELOPMENT, AS USUAL

Staff development follows some traditional formats. A common training day features a presenter or presenting team with a handsomely orchestrated presentation, well-developed thoughts that are interestingly featured on slides, and handouts for note taking. If the participants are fortunate enough they have been released with substitutes or by a scheduled nonstudent day for intense training. It all starts out with a high level of energy and expectations. There is coffee, tea, and possibly breakfast, with promises of lunch and an afternoon snack. Some time is given to housekeeping tasks, the presenter is introduced and the participants experience some kind of warm-up to alert them to the work that is ahead.

What often happens next is that a very important topic is introduced with a research base and delineation of a huge need for this information. Participant buy-in is generally high. The presenter completes one concept and moves directly into more depth by introducing more and more information. The receivers of the information are often asked to talk about what they have heard and how they can use the information. They may be encouraged to make a connection with what is happening in their classrooms. Then this cycle is repeated. Depending on the grade levels there could be as many as 20 sections filled with pertinent information for the participating teachers. By midafternoon the participants are full of evidence and thoughts of what they can use with their students. Laden with information and good thoughts of what they can try, they leave with ample notes and often an armload of materials, a resource list, or a book to read.

One of the districts that received the prestigious Race to the Top funds, for example, sponsored a common core teacher leader institute and many districts or consortiums offer this type of professional training. Institutes are designed to build capacity of teacher leaders, to support systemwide implementation of the common core, and to increase achievement of diverse learners. The institutes generally run for two days AND cover the topics of instructional strategies, curriculum, assessment, communication, collaboration, working with adult learners, system's thinking, working with protocols, building capacity of teacher leaders, content dissemination, and on and on. Most likely these are introductory topics with a variety of workshop choices. And this is a good example of the way teachers receive professional development. Another is a one-day seminar with all the teachers receiving the same information and experience.

Educators are willing to share their expertise, and learning foundations are providing a wealth of information over the Internet. One such training for teachers gives the PowerPoint slides through Wikispaces. It is produced by the Centers for Quality Teaching and Learning and covers critically important topics for implementation of the Common Core State Standards (CCSS). Topics presented include understanding and defining rigor for ELA, math with a rigorous framework, Bloom's Taxonomy, Webb's Depth of Knowledge chart and a rigor meter, samples of rigorous assessments, and 23 other equally important topics in a daylong training. The information is vital and well developed. It includes important tools teachers can use as they investigate the differences of the common core demands and what happened under the previous standards-based instruction. But it is too much, much too much, for one day of professional development! The wealth of information contained in this one-day session is enough for an entire year of topics that could be introduced, practiced, and put in place with classroom activities. How often are these two examples considered the standard for what teachers experience through seminars, institutes, and workshops?

Lost Impact From Training

After an all day in-service, teachers may have class the next day and some of the training pieces can be immediately put to use. The information from yesterday is already waning. The human brain can store information in working memory for about 24 hours, if that information was thought about, spoken about, experienced, or connected to previous experience. For new teaching practices to become part of a teacher's repertoire of professional skills and to be retrieved efficiently from long-term memory places, it will take practice and review, possibly feedback. Most likely, many of the topics presented at the previous training will become lost onto the pages of the handouts, unless there is a plan for immediate follow-up and implementation. After a week or so, if implementation has not occurred, memory for a huge percentage of the training day has lapsed. This cycle for professional development is repeated, even though research shows that the outcomes are minimal. With follow-up coaching, the results are better but still may not meet expectations.

Look to Teachers First

What could be different as the common core permeates districts is to look first at the instructional qualities teachers already bring to their positions. They are the ones who will make or break the common core. Teachers can be leaders *and* remain as teachers. Teachers can be learners and be the chief negotiators for the unique instructional shifts that are needed. Teachers can be leaders of students who are encouraged to learn with deeper understanding. Start with the teachers; they know what works. People who have moved into positions of management and administration may forget what it is like in the classroom. They become theoretical and at times unrealistic, because they may not be able to maintain a part of the action—in the classroom. Current research on teacher training indicates a strong pull toward teacher empowerment for change and innovation in teaching and learning.

Research and Professional Development

Teacher preparation is always a favorite topic for researchers and for teacher training colleges. There is no end to experts in this field. Now, there is an urgency to find the most recent and most effective practices as the common core is implemented.

Professional training for teachers can include an expansive list of activities: collegial interactions that range from formal nationally sponsored seminars to hallway discussions with other teachers. It is fortunate that there is a growing body of empirical research that suggests the features of effective professional development.

These core features that lead to teacher learning provide a starting point for assessing professional development programs, and they lead to a core conceptual framework for judging whether professional development is doing what we want it to do—increasing teacher knowledge and instruction in ways that translate into enhanced student achievement (Desimone, 2011, p. 28).

Embedded staff development, directly related to the work of teaching, has become a preferred practice for many in education. The opportunities are endless and may include designing curriculum, checking online resources, joining a teacher network, or self-examination of teaching preferences for learning outcomes. Sound familiar? This type of activity is exactly what is suggested in the previous chapters as student activities—a complex array of interrelated actions that result in increased learning for teachers, as it can for their students.

Core Professional Development Practices

Research and review of the literature identifies the core of professional development that is deemed to be effective. It includes focusing on **course content** and how students can learn the content. Teachers engage in **active learning** by analyzing student work, observing and providing feedback, or providing presentations rather than passively listening. Note the point here, *providing presentations,* because this is pivotal in this chapter. Another identified core issue is that of **coherence,** like coherence for the CCSS. For professional training, coherence means being in alignment with what has previously been learned, practices that match with beliefs, are consistent with school and district directions, and maintain a similarity with state and national reform movements. There is an agreement on

duration of training programs, as well. Most researchers encourage staff development that is extended over a minimum of a semester's work and has at least 20 hours of contact time. The final core feature involves **learning communities**, because teachers interact with others with common grades, subjects, or learning goals (Desimone, 2011).

This summary is pretty similar to what happened in the past. Basically, when staff development activities start with other people's ideas, teachers have been denied the opportunity to activate what they already know. Lieberman and Mace (2013) make a transformative proposal that training for teachers begins with practices teachers already use. When professional training begins with the skills teachers possess, they are invited into the conversation. They are included as they critique what is current, become open to new learning, and are willing to expand their repertoire of teaching tools. These researchers suggest that professional developers need to stop looking for the perfect training methods and look for what is presently successful in classrooms. These practices that are already productive can be expanded, revised, built on, and shared.

Staff development that is "homegrown" begins with teachers sharing at the local level, nourishing both themselves and their communities. These researchers also encourage accomplished teachers to "go public" with successful practices that have been refined over decades of teaching. The use of computers and educational networks helps educators exchange ideas about the layered, complex nature of learning for adults (and students) and allows them to build ties to a large network of professional learners.

STAFF DEVELOPMENT, RESPONDING TO THE COMMON CORE

While talking about a different professional development design, it is imperative to understand adult learners. Adults operate with a brain that is completely developed with a specialized design for learning. Although adults all have the same brain structures for learning, the way each brain is connected with neural networks is unique and individually based on life's experiences. Memory systems described in Chapter 4 are consciously and unconsciously operational. The adult learning system is efficient because it expedites information from one area of the brain to another for thought and response. Sometimes a mere word can set off an expansive explosion of ideas and thoughts that travel from one part of the brain to others instantaneously. To harness the endless opportunities for learning, adults make conscious decisions that limit themselves to preferences, which are useful and needed for the stage of life they are experiencing.

Teachers as Learners

Staff developers have known for a long time that novice teachers have different needs than those who are experienced teachers. In addition to variations in learning needs for teaching, differences in ages also have an impact on stages of social maturity. A teacher who has under 5 years of classroom teaching and also has family responsibilities with several children has a different need and tolerance for in-service than a teaching colleague who has 20 or more years in the classroom, has taught multiple grades, and has aspirations for leaving a mark on the teaching profession. The latter may be teaching classes at the university as a second position. Yet often all teachers are brought together to hear the same presentation and to react to the same information with small group interactions that are at the knowledge and comprehension discussion level.

Ages and Stages

There are other variations in teacher needs during professional development. One teacher may already be experienced in methods of a new innovation, while for another the process is totally new and there is no previous experience from which to draw. In the area of technology this type of difference has no relationship to age or years of teaching experience. An example is that this discussion will eventually lead to what Lieberman and Mace (2013) called "going public" with teacher training through the Internet. Younger, often less experienced teachers have more exposure to computer possibilities such as social networks and can adapt easily to an innovation with network sharing and learning. Teachers toward the end of their career may have no desire to put the effort into learning with computer networking.

The Adult Learning Cycle

Regardless of their enthusiasm toward or hesitancy to employ something new, all adults follow a common learning cycle. This type of cycle, represented in Figure 7.1, was conceptualized by Claxton and Murell (1987) to represent the classic work of John Dewey and Jean Piaget. Notice it begins with a **concrete experience**, such as observing and critiquing a new teaching practice, watching a video and planning with a peer for an innovative unit of study, or experiencing a new piece of equipment for physical education or the science lab. Following personal exposure, there is time for **reflective observation**, which could take many forms, such as talking it over, fitting the idea into something that already exists, or trying it individually several times to check the outcome. At this stage adults may reject, accept, or put the innovation on hold. To a large extent this decision can be influenced by life's experiences of values, beliefs, physical abilities, finances, or philosophies, to name a few. Many teaching innovations stall at this stage of learning and implementation. Assuming the innovation is accepted, the next phase of the cycle is for active engagement and experimentation. These activities lead the adult learner to the stage of **abstract conceptualization.** At this third level the learner understands the process or practice well enough to encourage others and to accurately describe how the new idea actually works. Finally, the **active experimentation** phase allows the learner to use the innovation in other situations and to use creative approaches to teach others.

Figure 7.1   The adult learning cycle begins with an experience and may end with active practice of a new skill or application of new learning

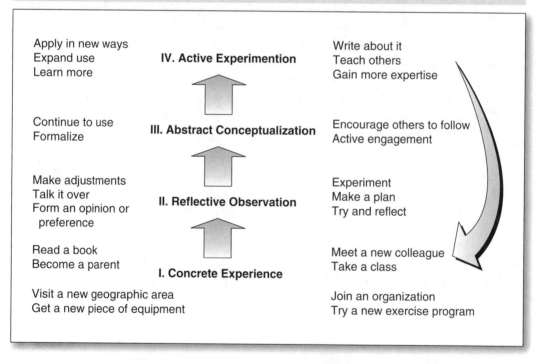

The adult learning cycle helps us identify teachers who are proficient in certain aspects of teaching and are ready to go public to share their expertise. They are the teachers who function in the active experimentation phases with many different areas of classroom practices. They are equipped with knowledge and steeped in experiences that help others unpack and implement innovations, such as the common core.

What can professional development look like to reach higher thinking levels for teachers, as well as for their students? Lesson planning questions in Chapter 5 are a good starting point to challenge teachers to think and produce at evaluative and synthesis levels of Bloom's Taxonomy. Teacher staff development can match these elevated levels, just as their work will help their students attain higher order thinking abilities.

Teachers as Leaders Among Their Peers

The stage has been set, and teachers are the actors. Effective professional development for the common core is identified by experts. It is teachers leading teachers, teachers being learners, teachers being leaders of their students. How does this challenge teachers to behave in expanded ways for professional development? The leadership choice was defined by Gabriel in 2005, long before education was thinking "common core." He identified the school administrator, who is positioned to guide the school toward its goals, but holds teachers as those who possess the powerful strategies toward improving student achievement.

Teachers want to be a part of something as significant as the CCSS. They want to be contributing members. Nurturing teacher leaders is not only a current and effective way to provide professional development, but it also creates a greater sense of ownership, buy-in, and community building. Most school leaders step forward without special compensation; rather they contribute for the reward of leadership itself. They feel a sense of self-worth from being heard and by serving their colleagues in addition to their students.

Professional Learning—Professionals Leading

For an example of teachers as leaders, Sammamish High is once again in the spotlight. At this school teachers are asked to examine their entire course at one time, not lesson by lesson. They are challenged to start with the big picture:

- redesign course elements,
- increase student ownership in learning,
- creatively link their content to real disciplines outside the school, and
- identify contemporary problems for their students to tackle.

They work in design teams that allow them to learn from each other, focus on what students experience, and deepen their own reflective practice. This work happens during one period each day through released time.

Teacher Release Time

Talk about time. How can school teams have time to work together for one period a day, if there is not a grant to fund it? When the focus is dramatically turned from teacher performance to student learning, school leaders can find time to work together. First, they ask some questions about school practices that create barriers to making the time they require for planning, collaborating, and strengthening student learning (see Table 7.1).

After responding to these questions, school teams investigate practices that can be more time effective. They look to see if another plan may provide a better learning environment for students and time for teachers to work together. The common core demands different student learning outcomes. It also demands that teachers see themselves differently, see the school where they teach with new eyes, and see each other as resources for new ways of doing school.

Teachers as Leaders for Student Learning

Teachers know and they can suggest changes to teaching practices that are not effective for student deep learning. And, there are some outspoken experts that help direct them to challenge some ideas that are long standing. A former school administrator and current consultant, Mike

Table 7.1   Questions School Teams Can Ask to Find Ways to Create Time for Teachers to Collaborate and Plan

Tough Questions to Answer and Consider
1. Why do we stay with traditional time periods?
2. Do we take advantage of bell-to-bell instruction and learning, or is the first part of the class, which is the best learning time, spent with housekeeping tasks?
3. Are there flex periods that meet student needs and free up some of our teachers?
4. How effective is study hall? The computer lab?
5. Does learning happen in the community? If so, how is that time used? Is it efficient?
6. How is technology used as an effective way for students to learn rote memory skills that require drill and practice?
7. What are some ways that large groups of students could be engaged with learning with fewer teachers?
8. What community resources, businesses, or volunteers are available to increase student-to-adult ratios?
9. How could teacher workshops during summer be funded?

Schmoker (2001), expresses his concerns about schools and works to help ferret out some of the inherent problems. He identifies the single greatest deterrent of learning, not as socioeconomic factors or funding levels—rather it is instruction. Two "hot topic" areas of classroom instruction that beg for teachers to evaluate and design teacher led training are direct instruction versus indirect instruction and differentiated instruction.

Elementary Reading and Direct Instruction

It is not uncommon for administrators, consultants, or visitors to elementary classrooms to see activities during reading instruction that are only faintly related to reading. Schmoker (2001) refers to classrooms with these sidebar activities as "Crayola classrooms." Children are working in small groups doing busy work while the small group gathered around the teacher is receiving direct instruction to tackle the task of training the brain to develop a pathway for proficient reading. First, it is accepted that students learn to read with a sequenced, complete reading program that is designed for direct instruction. When teachers group students by ability it means two or three groups are waiting for or have already finished their instruction, and they may spend up to three-fourths of their reading instruction time period doing work that may or may not improve their ability to read. In primary grades many schools assign up to 2.5 hours to reading instruction. What is important here is to plan as well for the students who are not with the teacher as for those who are.

Children need to read more, and there are many ways to increase their time with books or readers. Notice the activities from this list that are directly related to instruction without direct contact with the teacher.

- Read with a volunteer, older child, or peer to practice vocabulary, answer important questions, or practice fluency.
- Listen to a tape recording, read along, and tell what you have read to your partner.
- Use computer programs for word identification and reading practice with progress monitoring.
- Practice reading and rereading a book with decodable words and sight words that are known in order to develop fluency skills. This may be a partner read.
- Silent, independent reading to answer "big questions."
- Read and write. After reading, write two paragraphs that you will read to your group to help them see pictures of what you read and learned.

(Continued)

(Continued)

- Read and find the new vocabulary. Give your definition for each.
- Read and discuss. After reading meet with your group to prepare the best answers possible to the big questions.
- Free reading with a direct purpose, for example, find out which pet would be good for your family and explain your choice, or if you traveled to Minnesota, which states would you pass and what is the preferred way you would travel? Why?

School has a limited number of hours, and the time for classroom activities must be maximized, not filled with work to keep students busy. Time designated for reading needs to be spent bell to bell with reading related activities. An expanded view of direct instruction in the early years needs to fill a major part of the time children have to learn to read.

Secondary Reading and Indirect Instruction

During the secondary years there is decreased direct instruction and increased time for focused indirect work times. Interestingly, some of the activities listed above can be modified to work for older students, as well. Students who are not reading at grade level have more direct instruction and focused reading activities. Those who are accomplished readers work on independent reading, reading searches and inquiry, and developing responses to big questions.

Several studies have shown that having students read an additional 280,000 words per year can mean the difference between scoring at the 20th percentile and scoring at the 50th. That's like reading two books the length of a Harry Potter novel (about 155,000 words) (Schmoker, 2001).

This topic of instruction for reading provides a good starting place for teachers working together. Effective practices can be identified and validated, while those that just keep children busy can be eliminated. Identification of a variety of reading activities requires intense planning, but stops short of what is known as *differentiated instruction*.

Differentiated Instruction

As it currently is viewed, some argue that differentiated instruction was never fully warranted as an effective educational intervention. There is validation for continual assessment of students and meeting them where they are with instruction. And an underpinning implicit theory that different students have different ways of learning. Yes and no. Children each have unique maps of connections to the structures of the brain designed for learning and remembering. However, all children have basically the same brain structures that are stimulated for learning. Teachers must pay attention to the unique way each child understands and learns to remember. However, children, as unique as they are, will all profit from good instructional practices, whether they are exposed individually, in a small group, or with whole class instruction. That is a broad statement and should not be interpreted, after all that has been presented in previous chapters, to mean whole class instruction will suffice. Instead, it depends on what the curriculum outcomes require. The point is a good teacher will know how to group students in ways that maximize learning. See Chapter 5 for a variety of ways students can work in groups or on their own.

Possibly it is the term differentiated instruction that sends educators into a frenzy of concern that they have to develop different lessons for each of their uniquely learning students. Actually, when classroom projects themselves take on the level of sophistication required by the common core, there is room for students to self-differentiate. An example is given by Jennifer Stainton, a science department chair at Woodstock Union High School in Vermont. All 50 students in ninth grade completed a research project to measure levels of mercury in the environment. They collected dragonfly nymphs from a pond and samples of soil, leaf litter, and human hair. The project had so many parts that included developing questions, using and writing about the scientific method, creating posters, and making presentations that students with different abilities could all learn and succeed together (Pappano, 2011).

Implementation of the CCSS may indeed help teachers as they work together on big learning tasks. Teachers looking together at the instruction needed and the tasks to be assigned can then ascertain that students of all levels can be successful.

Close the Gap

Implementation of the common core is the right time to close the differences between what is known and what is done to increase student learning. All signs point to teachers, full of capacity and working together, as the straight way to achieving common core expectations. Teachers need the opportunity to redesign school schedules and find regular times they can work together to develop, refine, and approach instruction that looks first at desired student outcomes. And then to have regular times to honor and celebrate eminent successes as students become more engaged with learning, gain an excitement about what they do at school, and produce at deeper levels of understanding.

It is not enough for teachers to form learning communities, operate in collaborative teams, and make dramatic changes in the classroom. This chapter, with its focus on teachers, is followed with one that puts structure to professional development design and to its implementation school by school, district by district for the CCSS.

Systems Change

Americans invest in their public education system for the common good of their country. The overarching goal is for national prosperity with stable families and communities. Current social, political, and economic changes make learning success and shaping moral character for the nation's children more critical than ever. An approach for school or district level adjustment cannot be the same mission and goal process that has been used in the past. Now is the time to take a new look at how school systems can change to accommodate student learning and social development in a free country through the common core standards. It needs to happen day by day, systematically and incrementally at the school campuses, with leadership and support from colleagues at districts, counties, teacher preparation institutions, and state departments of education. Districts are already navigating pathways for professional development with network teams. How does a district road map look that values instructional shifts and promotes teachers as leaders?

Education Is Valued

Students of today must be prepared for the variety of adult roles that await them as citizens, parents, employees or employers, leaders, volunteers, entrepreneurs, and futuristic designers. To achieve their potential as adults, young people need a range of skills and knowledge that comes from a large variety of school subjects. The organizational leaders who designed the Common Core State Standards (CCSS) demand that schools prepare high school graduates for 21st-century skills. These skills beg for students to develop abilities for self-management, so they are equipped for problem solving through critical, evaluative thinking. They need to be armed with effective communication abilities and to be capable of highly inventive thinking. It is widely accepted that the current system of education must revamp to meet these lofty but attainable goals.

These tall orders require education to once again undergo a massive systems change. The last 20 years of adjustments to the school system have not resulted in substantial differences for most students who go through the system. The school system has remained relatively the same at most of the nation's schools. This request for something different must be just that—something recognizably different with outstandingly different outcomes to develop agile, flexible learners.

Major culture shift in the way instruction is delivered begins with acceptance of already established and commonly held values. Citing the purpose for and imposing great value on the education of future citizens begins with the nation's department of education. The intent and impact of the national system filters through state departments of education and are ultimately reflected in local district statements of mission and goals. While keeping the values that have always made America's school system prestigious, school can look, feel, and be different, when the spotlight is focused on what, where, and how students learn. For example, one district's response to the federal level and industrial leader's push to produce 21st-century learners is to create learning environments that are designed to improve learning and teaching. Charleston County School District in South Carolina puts a focus on personalized strategies for career and college. By looking at needs for the end of public education, post high school, this district has aligned tools and supports for students and their teachers to meet the new standards of the common core.

Learning Is a Performance

It is time for education to reflect a system that is specifically designed for student learning. The stage and the drama of how school is done can be performed in new ways. Teachers are removed from center stage and from being the main performer. Students fill the stage as the teacher moves from acting to the role of director of learning. The entire scene must change from the telling teacher to the directing teacher, who acts as a leader for students as performers. Students in response to the common core are the actors, the ones now in the spotlight. Their work is critical to the outcome and review of a new venue in drama.

LEADERSHIP AND STUDENT LEARNING

Research continually acknowledges building principals as the second most important position after classroom teachers, to influence student learning outcomes. In a classic study the Wallace Foundation with the University of Toronto and the University of Minnesota reviewed educational literature to arrive at some qualities of leaders that are pertinent today. A report by Leithwood and colleagues (2004) identified three expectations of effective leaders: (1) setting direction, (2) developing people, and (3) supporting the work of the organization. The last one enlists an entire range of conditions and incentives that are provided at the district and school level that aim at support for teachers and students for positive learning outcomes.

The literature review addressed options for organizational change that have relevance to the transitions needed for the common core. A focus for change can be at different levels:

- the total school system,
- one school at a time,
- one curricula (RLA, mathematics, STEM, science), or
- innovative approaches to instruction.

While different leadership styles were addressed in the report, which was produced a decade ago, the Wallace Foundation has continued to support educational systems to improve student learning outcomes. Their website provides videos of principals describing how they supported positive change for teachers and students. One presenter, Kevin Tashlein, tells how students responded to the school's Standards of Excellence by developing a marketing campaign for other students to get on board and take responsibilities for their own learning. Another, Baretta Wilson, provided staff collaborative time by giving up weekly faculty meetings and switching from a seven- to an eight-period day. Focusing on teaching strategies that worked for the top 50% of the students to meet the needs of the bottom 50 was a strategy used by Mikel Royal. The Wallace Foundation (2013) is a viable resource for district and school leaders. In addition to providing endless current publications, Wallace works with states and school districts to seek better ways for professional training, hiring practices, principal support and evaluation, and evaluation of other key figures in schools.

Soft, Definite Systems Change

Anyone who has been in education for a while has lived through strategic planning for change at their schools or school system. The process of defining the change by a strategic plan can take on a life of its own. It can become overwhelmingly time demanding. By the time all the stakeholders have been retooled and all the resources are in place, there is little teacher enthusiasm left to actually attain the conceptual and active experimentation levels needed to make the change apparent in classroom activities and for its target outcomes, capable learners.

Realize there are books and entire university courses that direct transforming change in schools. Current publications and electronic contacts are provided in the list of resources. The intent of this chapter is to provide a workable description of what happens for systemic, yet incremental change. Different from change in the past, which has been developmental or transitional, the outcome of this progressive effort is a subtle and steady upending of the traditional school experience. Previous changes in education have placed emphasis on the experience of change, working through the planning process. Change required now is nothing short of transformational. The process, happening daily, incrementally, revamps classrooms. The process for redirection for the *how* of teaching is the desired outcome, but it cannot happen instantaneously.

Daily activities must go on. It is not about the process of change, it is about the changes that occur for students as a result of the process. Modifications can be as simple as **beginning instruction immediately at the start of the teaching period**, not using valuable teaching time to take role, collect homework, and do other housekeeping actions. This change by itself speaks volumes about what school is about, and it has to do with learning. Changes can happen on a daily basis and do not have to wait for a teachers' guide, the new curriculum materials, student resources, or the new school year. Teachers can begin **having students teach what they have learned** to another group of students, for example, without major variation to the instructional plan. Implementing student-focused learning can begin the very next day after teachers accept and switch their thinking from their performance to what students are doing.

Remember, however, the effect of this type of change experience is unknown as the process is undertaken. There are no predefined solutions; they evolve during the process. Individuals involved experience changes in mindset, behavior, and even make personal and cultural adjustments. Gradually, simple, initial teaching behavioral changes develop into novel sets of teaching skills and tools.

What Districts Are Doing

Previously mentioned, Race to the Top is a federally funded program distributing $400 million to 16 selected districts and consortiums. Recipients exhibit abilities and plans to provide innovative approaches to education. Target areas include to personalize and deepen student learning, directly improve student achievement and educator effectiveness, close achievement gaps, and prepare every student to succeed in college and their careers (U.S. Department of Education, 2013).

What is already happening in some of the selected districts? Superintendent Karen Schauer used the Internet to share a special message with her administrators and teachers from the Galt Joint Union School District in California. The district developed a Student Learning Framework organized around three simple, yet critical focus questions.

1. What do we want students to learn and be able to do?

2. How do we know if they learned it?

3. What are we going to do about it if they don't learn it or are proficient?

These questions center teacher thinking as they reflect individually, work together through collective inquiry, and develop strategic actions (Schauer, 2013).

Another California district, Lindsay Unified, has been developing a performance-based assessment system for the last 4 years. They are recognized as a pace-setter for the rest of the nation's students for personalized mastery learning. Additional information about Lindsay Unified located in the References and Further reading section located at the end of the book.

Sammamish High School in Washington, allowed 5 years for process development as they transferred practices and behaviors to develop a problem-based learning (PBL) school. They schedule 5 days of staff development during summers for institutes run by their own teachers. They create time to work together, even at times by having multiple teachers in classrooms. Teachers lead their students through the content to be learned, and then students become leaders, creatively processing activities during the learning episode. Their teacher's role may be described as creator, designer, reviewer, and implementer as students become learners who can describe and teach what they are learning. More about Sammamish High School can also be found in the references at the end of this book.

Guilford County Schools in North Carolina won a $30 million Race to the Top grant. Administrators determined to use the money to create and stimulate student-led learning in 24 middle schools. Students are using fewer textbooks and the district plans for them to work with educational software loaded onto a tablet device. Through this program, student progress toward mastering common core concepts will be continually monitored. More information about Guilford's Race to the Top grant is available in the reference section. Although these examples are interesting and innovative, there are a multitude of creative responses to a new way of doing education, possibly the reader is in the middle of one of them.

Focus on Student Learning

It may seem that adjusting the educational focus from what the teacher does to how the students learn, with support from neuroscience, is just a good idea. An idea it is not. A shift of this magnitude is based on years of research, dismal student outcomes, and system and teacher disappointment. A dramatic correction to the way school is done has potential to see results of increased student interest, involvement, amplified production, and deep, enriched thinking skills. To change human practice and behavior some key structures must be in place. It is not a neat sequence of activities that encourages educators to embrace a new course of action for a district, a school, a grade level, or within a department. Work to advance the changes needed for the common core can continue to evolve over weeks, months, and years. And those involved need to know there can be some messy times.

Include All Stakeholders

Who are the stakeholders? At the onset it is those who are not only responsible but also passionate to change the way classroom instruction happens. Generally, the change is instrumented at the district or school level. At some schools a group of teachers may come forward with an innovative plan that needs support from the building principal or district level personnel. While it is most likely conversations will begin at the district level, remember this is untidy business and may not always follow expected routes. A leadership group begins the conversation and works through questions, such as these:

1. What do we envision for our system (grade level, department, school, or district)?

2. Define the change drivers that propel this transformation (e.g., environmental forces, industry, organization or government requirements, and changes to the product [student] desired outcomes).

3. What are we currently doing that matches what we envision?

4. What actions, behaviors, and beliefs will be different from what we are currently doing?

5. What student outcome benefits can be expected?

6. Who else needs to be involved?

7. How and when do we include more people?

Taking the steps needed to focus on learning-centered classrooms can emerge initially by defining the educational values people hold. Defining values that drive people in their daily work is an intense experience. It may be assumed that everyone on the educational team has the same or similar sets of values. When conversation begins with Question 1, similarities and big picture commonalities are voiced. However, during the activity, interesting variations tend to emerge. Participants are requested to expand their thinking to new possibilities for their role in student learning. As common ideas meld into usable statements, stakeholders experience the opportunity to form relationships and begin to understand each other better.

DISTRICT ROADMAP OF SUPPORT

Think of the difference a district can make for its principal leaders and its teachers when it adapts a new or expanded vision of support that is truly transformational. Just as it is proposed that the teacher is not on center stage, the players are the students, the district role can adjust, as well. In this "new order of doing," the district office exists to support teachers as they revision and retool. A response that lightens the load placed on teachers allows them to increase their energies to student learning. The district office personnel work to support what is happening in the classroom with these actions:

- Provide clearly defined values and statements of direction.
- Communicate the organizational system.
- Define and articulate required county, state, and federal requirements.
- Safeguard finances and provide adequate funding to attract promising teachers and supply stellar instructional supports.

- Define clearly stated responsibilities to students, their parents, teachers and schools.
- Deliver instructional support services.
- Provide a personnel system with clearly defined job descriptions, well-defined hiring practices, and evaluation systems.*
- Organize dynamic professional development teams.

*Note: See *Next Generation Teacher Evaluation* by Marzano and Toth (2013).

This list is ginormous with simple statements. Each could represent the work of entire departments, depending on the size of the school district. For example, delivering instructional support services includes resource personnel, professional support and training, district level meetings and opportunities, curriculum plans, meaningful professional development, a communication system, basic supplies, and a transportation plan. What is important is that supports are in place and district office personnel voice their stake in the mission of instruction for students. All levels of personnel in the district, as well as at the schools, can see themselves as a huge team of stakeholders. They value their work and see their place in the overarching district design. And through a clear plan all members of the district or schools work to prepare the most valued resource, the students.

Social Relationships and Educational Change

Alan J. Daly (2010) sums up the work of educational change and personal relationships in his book, *Social Network Theory and Educational Change*. He claims it is not the technical plans and blueprints that determine the success or failure of educational reform. Rather it is the social and relational ties among the stakeholders that support or constrain the direction, timing, and depth of the movement. It has long been accepted that an instructional leader, such as the district superintendent or the building principal has three leadership dimensions: (1) claiming and proclaiming the mission, (2) managing the instructional program, and (3) promoting a positive organizational climate. Add to this mix the opportunity for and support of distributed leadership and the organization called school has dimensions for change that are not only possible but also sustainable.

Support and Resources

Foundational support is multifaceted and readily available for grant funding and for consultant services. During research for this book, many were explored and are listed in the section References and Further Reading.

Websites to identify resources for instructional practices, teachers as leaders, teacher and administrator evaluation, and problem-based learning, for example, are readily available simply by typing a topic and doing a web search. To keep a pulse on what teachers are experiencing, various social and professional sites and blogs exist for teachers to share successful practices and to ask when help is needed. Districts have set up their own internal web systems to give announcements; provide calendar information, books and electronic reading, and instructionally related videos; to communicate new information; and to support professional and staff interactive communication throughout the organization.

Some resources that may not have been previously identified are supplied here. They are listed without consideration of priority and are not endorsed by the author or publisher.

- *The William and Flora Hewlett Foundation*, Education Program, provides grants to increase economic opportunity and civic engagement by educating students to succeed in a changing world through deeper learning.
- *Thomas B. Fordham Institute* includes an extensive list of funding institutes and organizations.
- *The Noyce Foundation* maintains a goal to help young people become curious, thoughtful, and engaged learners by getting them excited about science with programs outside of school.
- *The Clayton Christenson Institute for Disruptive Innovation* uses theories of innovation to drive academic research for problems that vex society.
- *Partnership Institute for Mathematics and Science Education Reform*, University of Kentucky and Noyce Foundation and New Tech West, Ohio promote the education of science, technology, engineering, and mathematics (STEM).
- *U.S. Department of Education*, Race to the Top Grants provide district and consortium awards for innovative practices.
- *Educurious* combines project-based learning, technology, and connections with real-world experts to capture the imagination and interest of today's students.
- *The GE Foundation* is the philanthropic organization of GE that works to solve some of the world's most difficult problems, health, education, the environment, and disaster relief.
- *Transformative Inquiry Design for Effective Schools* (TIDES) partners with district and key school decision makers to find team-oriented solutions for students in this rapidly changing society.
- *The Khan Academy* provides a free world-class education in the areas of math, biology, chemistry, physics, finance, history, and the

humanities. This is a self-paced way for individuals to obtain an education or can be used by teachers or tutors to design a unique program for their students. It can be a part of an innovative educational plan and would not be suggested as a total learning program under the common core.

- *The Curriculum Corner* weaves the common core into classroom practices and is a good teacher resource.

This initial list is far from being exhaustive but gives an indication of the vast support that is available for education systems.

Still to Be Resolved

There are major considerations that have not been resolved for implementation and for success of the Common Core State Standards. First, obviously the present teacher workforce has not been retooled to teach in a way that fosters deep learning for students. Organization and scheduling at schools are in many ways incompatible with teaching and learning requirements. An initial blush of responses is for the good of all students, but educational systems and their teachers know that delivery of educational services cannot target all students with the same methodologies. Organizations that advocate for and support the education of students with special needs participated in the development of the CCSS. But educators know the needs of students who learn differently have not been adequately addressed. Children who present unique individual, socio-economic, cultural, and learning abilities need varied learning platforms for the delivery of educational services.

Substantially more financial resources for more teachers along with up-to-date learning materials and laboratories need to be provided. Older school buildings need renovating, old ways of thinking need to be updated, and often teaching materials need to be replenished. An effort to correct educational inequities and move the system toward future needs is already seen from a large number of foundations that have selected education as a target for grants and funding.

Problems and Answers

There are problems and there are answers. There is no easy way to uproot the education process and neatly plant it to grow differently. The stakeholders are many, and the mission is vital. The pathway is varied, but the future can be secure for students to be prepared as thinkers, questioners, discoverers, and innovators. A soft change approach for incremental successes can be instituted from the perception changes developed in this publication.

- Embrace the science of neurology to understand deep student learning.
- Focus on students and what they can do to learn.
- Define teachers as those who are responsible for providing the core curriculum and directing learning activities.
- Look to district offices and other overseer organizations to provide vision, structure, and a definition of the system for education.
- Use teacher expertise and experience to lead teaching reform.
- Secure trust in the organization, school, district, county, state, and federal education system by defining and providing support systems that are directly felt in classrooms.

The giant expectations for a new way of doing education under the CCSS require powerful thinking, but there are a gigantic number of great minds who are fired up to find solutions.

Explain the Learning Brain

Curious readers who want to understand why a focus on learning makes sense can develop a deeper understanding about the brain in this chapter. Phrases and concepts influenced by neurology, brain science, are identified in previous chapters and are explained with a more scientific interpretation here. Numbers in parenthesis indicate chapters where the term is introduced.

Adult Brains Designed To Learn (2, 7)—During the school years students are exposed to and are involved with many different ways of learning. Each time something new is learned, it requires the hippocampus located in the central, core region of the brain to hold the information until it is understood at the automatic level. When automaticity occurs new learning is stored elsewhere in the brain. By the time a young adult reaches brain maturity, the brain has become efficient at determining what practice and rehearsal activities are most successful. Learning habits that were least successful have diminished, and neural networks supporting unsuccessful practices have atrophied and died. The adult brain is a smooth, effective operator to learn for life.

Adult Learner Insights (2, 7)—A study by Dr. Russell Poldrack and colleague (2004) at University of California, Los Angeles, revealed that adults can sustain a thought by using mature executive control and attention systems that are not available to children. The researcher used functional magnetic resonance imaging (fMRI) to observe what areas of the brain were active during a learning episode. He observed how the adult subjects responded to questions, and he determined that adults are not good at being able to describe how they learn. And they are not good predictors of how well they will remember and recall (Nevills & Wolfe, 2009). If adults have a hard time understanding themselves as learners, how can it be expected they will be learning experts if they happen to be teachers?

Attention Deficit Hyperactivity Disorder (ADHD) (4)—A recent study examined brain connectivity networks forming prior to birth by screening women in the later stages of pregnancy. A functional MRI, which measures the flow of blood and oxygen in the brain, was used to study the brain development of 29 fetal brains between 24 to 38 weeks gestation. The researchers stated that common brain disorders, such as ADHD and autism, are thought to be the result of abnormalities in the way the brain forms networks for connectivity when the child is still in utero (Posani, 2013).

Basic Brain Structures (4, 5)—

- Basal Ganglia—subcortical nuclei located under the brain's motor cortex that modulate stimuli, regulate actions for movement, and control the flow of information into working memory.
- Cerebral Cortex—the deeply folded outer layers of the brain that are also called the neocortex. The combination of areas, lobes, and cortices is responsible for the feats of the brain that make humans unique: for example, executive thought, critical thinking, awareness of emotion, and deep learning.
- Corpus Callosum—a bundle of large myelinated fibers (axons) that connect the left to the right hemisphere of the human brain.
- Frontal Lobes—areas of the right and left hemispheres located directly above the eyes and extending to the back of the ears. These areas of the cerebral cortex are responsible for executive function requiring the highest level of human thinking.
- Glial Cells—cells tinier and more numerous than neurons act as stimulators, nursemaids, and clean-up crew members for neurons. There are different types of glial cells, each with a specific purpose. One type attaches itself to the axons of neurons and creates a myelin sheath. When neurons for a specific task have become myelinated, the brain system or memory for big thoughts becomes efficient and speedy during the thought process.
- Hippocampus—small left and right hemisphere structures that are located in the limbic system, the primitive part of the human brain.

Neuroscientists discovered that they function as the place for working memory. New potential learning activates these structures until the learning is dropped from memory or moved to another area of the brain for permanent recall (long-term memory).

- Limbic System—the innermost core of the human brain and the brains of animals, as well. This system of structures responds to emotionally charged input and can react at an unconscious level, even to the point of overriding the executive, thinking function of the brain.

- Motor Cortex—also called the motor strip, this band of specialized neurons receives and sends messages to the muscular system for both conscious and unconscious responses.

- Occipital Lobes—right and left hemisphere structures that are located under the back of the skull. They receive images from the eyes and interpret what is being seen with the help of the visual association area and long-term memory areas that provide the names of and a complete picture of the images seen.

- Olfactory Areas—areas of the cerebral cortex located between the eyes and responds to smells from the environment. It is the first area of the five senses to complete its development and is ready to receive input at birth.

- Sensory Cortex—also called the somatosensory cortex, this band of fibers is located at the foremost part of the parietal lobes. It receives and interprets parietal input, including touch, sight, and hearing.

- Temporal Lobes—areas of the cerebral cortex located above the ears that receive auditory input and interact with the parietal and occipital lobes for interpretation and association of sounds.

- Thalamus—a receiving station located in the center of the limbic system. It receives and filters input from the sensory cortex for danger prior to sending it back to an association area for interpretation. The thalamus is also the pleasure center of the brain. Dopamine, a neurotransmitter that is produced during pleasurable experiences, affects the thalamus and the body has a sense of pleasure and a desire to maintain the happy feeling (See Figure 9.1 and 9.2).

Emotional System (4)—When it comes to emotions, humans use the same structures and the same responses as animals do. Humans act and respond first then cognitively assess the situation. Often called *fight or flight*, it is the rush or surge of energy that automatically transfigures all response systems when a threat is perceived, even before a person consciously knows what is happening. If the senses receive alarming input, the thalamus reacts and instantaneously alerts the amygdala. The

Figure 9.1   The Brain's Main Lobes and Cortices

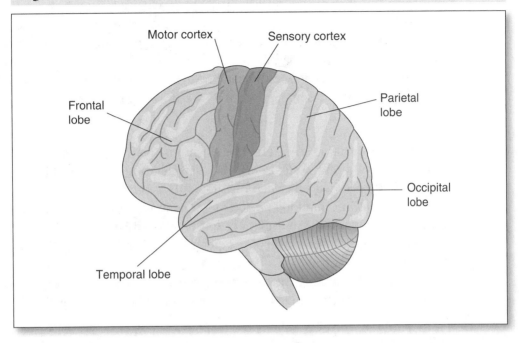

Figure 9.2   The Thalamus, a Way Station to Receive Input From the Senses

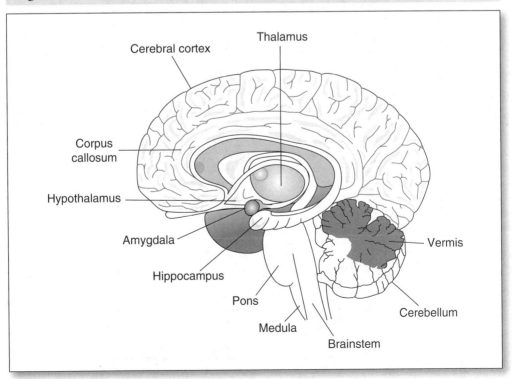

amygdala activates the muscular system, the heart for increased blood flow, and the thyroid and other chemical producing structures. Food digestion stops and an initial decrease of blood flow to the brain is experienced. Essentially the amygdala has overridden the powerful executive function of the frontal lobes, as the person responds in survival mode. A short while into the episode the person regains cognitive function and thinks through what is happening and how the body in its anxious state is responding.

Filtering Systems (4, 5)—The human brain has both conscious and unconscious filtering systems. Unconscious filtering happens through specially assigned neurons when the thalamus in the primitive section of the brain drops information and does not send it on to the cerebral cortex for interpretation. Most information that is received is lost as if it never happened: a cough, the sound of the computer running, a slight discomfort of being hungry, a flash of an ad on the side of the computer screen, the feel of one's shoes, or the weight of a cell phone in a pocket. If something is important enough to receive attention, a phone ringing, growling

Figure 9.3 The thalamus and the amygdala located in the limbic system can override the frontal lobes when students feel unsafe in the classroom.

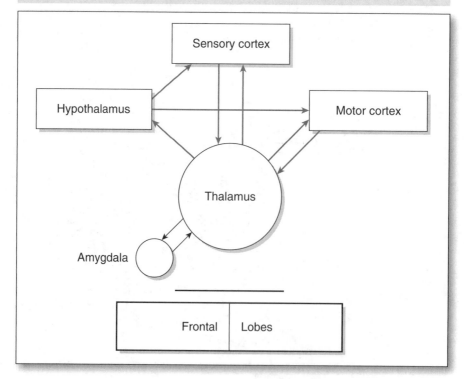

stomach, or, for example, feeling cold, the person may give the input a slight response, but not attempt to remember that it happened. These reactions show a conscious decision that the input was not important enough to hold in working memory. In the classroom the teacher gives some information and students may pay attention. Some consciously mull it over and want to remember it. Others may make a decision that it is unimportant to them and treat it as if it was never heard. Unconscious or consciously the human brain continues to filter information to protect itself from remembering everything. There is just too much important information that needs to be stored, so filtering systems protect people from overloading their brains with minutia. See Figure 9.4 to picture how the thalamus, frontal lobes, and basal ganglia work both consciously and unconsciously to protect the brain from overload.

How Much Learning Is Remembered (2)—It depends on the interest of the learner, the intensity of the sensory stimuli, and the need of the learner to use the information at another time. Learners lose much of the

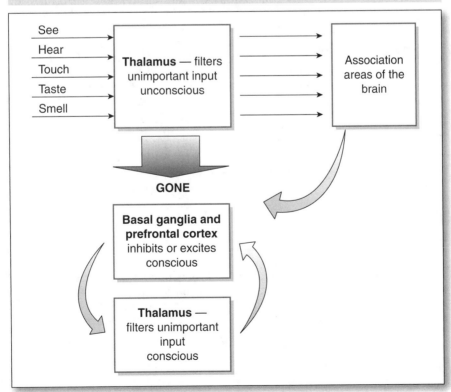

Figure 9.4   Diagram of the Brain's Systems for Filtering Information With the Thalamus (Unconscious) and Basal Ganglia Systems

information presented to them if they do not consciously decide to think about and to reflect on it.

Memory Systems (4)—Two basic long-term memory systems describe how learners recognize, remember, recall, react, and recite: Declarative (*what* is remembered) and Nondeclarative (*how* to respond to a task). See Figure 9.5.

- *Declarative memory*—Explicit, conscious memory that allows information to be stored in an organized manner, and subsequently recalled by speaking, writing, or listening. It has two sub parts: semantic and episodic.
  - *Semantic memory* is words, phrases, sentences, or any other form of text that is recalled and articulated through talking or writing. As a part of the declarative memory system, it reflects the learner's background information and experience.
  - *Episodic Memory* is long-term memory of a happening or occurrence that elicits strong emotions.

- *Procedural, Nondeclarative memory*—Unconscious responses to a question, task, or request that require the learner to know the process or

Figure 9.5 Long term memory has two distinct systems, declarative and procedural.

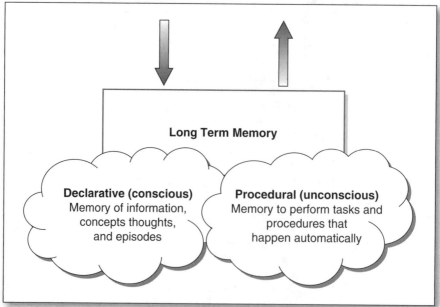

Figure 9.6   A complete traditional model of the memory systems beginning with input from the sensory system with a small amount of important information transferring into working memory where information is manipulated until it moves to permanent storage through the conscious declarative system or the unconscious procedural system

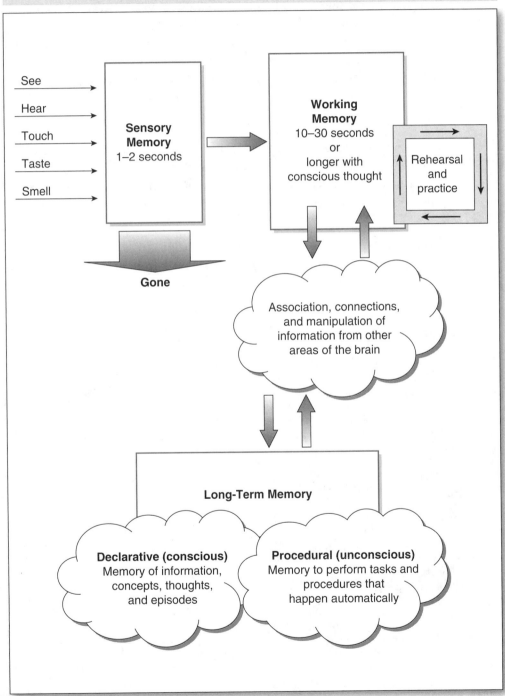

answer spontaneously. This type of memory usually requires exceptional practice for the cerebellum to perform the process with automaticity. It has two sub parts: procedural and rote.

○ *Procedural memory* is a nondeclarative memory system that allows learners to unconsciously conduct a process, such as reading, walking, singing, and speaking.

○ *Rote memory* is a part of the nondeclarative memory system that elicits responses almost unconsciously. It can be a spontaneous response to a question or instantaneous recognition of a word, an object, a sound, a taste, or a smell.

Neurons—Nerve cells in the brain and central nervous system are called *neurons*. Their job is to preform connections between one neuron's axon and other neurons' dendrites throughout the central nervous system. There are many sizes and shapes of neurons depending on their location in the system.

Neuron Networks (4)—Nerve cells, neurons, are stimulated by electrical charges to become unstable and to spew chemicals called *neurotransmitters* into a tiny gap, the synapse, between one neuron's axon and

Figure 9.7

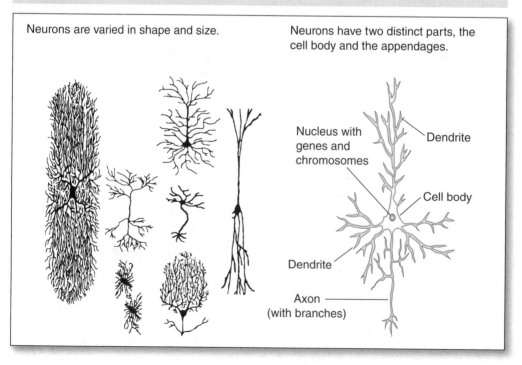

Neurons are varied in shape and size.

Neurons have two distinct parts, the cell body and the appendages.

Nucleus with genes and chromosomes

Dendrite

Cell body

Dendrite

Axon (with branches)

other neurons' dendrites, which in turn electrically stimulate an array of other neurons. However, it is not one neuron to its surrounding neighbor neurons that results in learning. Rather it is tens of thousands of neurons responding to a learner's single thought. The more the learner thinks about and engages with an idea or concept the more connections among neurons develop. And, if the learner visits this information many times, the neurons develop a network of nerve cells that can instantaneously be activated and connected to information already stored in long-term memory. Rather than traveling like on a rocky, dirt

Figure 9.8 Neurons communicate chemically across a synaptic channel and electrically within the neuron body.

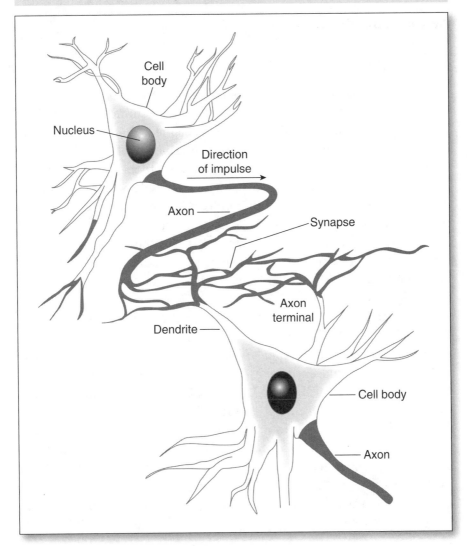

road, neuron networks are activated with speed and efficiency like driving on a super autobahn.

Neuroplasticity (2, 4)—One of the many amazing features of the human brain is that it constructs and connects itself based on input from the environment. Although it is often talked about how much children learn during childhood, the adult brain is far from being hard-wired. The adult brain system for processing new information is complete at the end of adolescence. It is a smooth operation as it receives, accepts or declines, processes new information, and determines where it goes for storage. Areas for new learning continue to become more complex with each new experience.

Neuroscience Provides Answers (2)—

Why do some children learn successfully,
while others in the same classroom repeatedly fail?

This is one of the BIG questions for neuroscientists and their teaching colleagues. There are some answers, but we will continue to learn more about learning, similar to the design for deep learning in the common core. We have answers, but the answers are not complete and will continue to develop in time. So here are two responses to this question: (1) Not only is each child's brain connected differently based on their experiences, but also physiologically, some children have brains that process information more rapidly than others. (2) While some of the processing time has to do with heredity, children can be prompted to respond with more speed. Practices such as giving rapid responses to simple questions, identification of vocabulary, or math facts can encourage children to speed up thinking processing (Wolf, 2007).

Another issue for learning happens at the neurological level and is studied through the specific field of epigenetics. Scientists have unlocked secrets of DNA that are located within the nucleus of the neurons. Some children have a genetic disposition for chromosomes that are tightly wrapped around the learning proteins, called *histones*. When this situation occurs it is difficult for learning to stick, or be recorded in the brain. Certain neurons that were designed for learning tasks simply are impregnable and do not respond even in ideal learning circumstances (Levine, 2008). Children with this learning problem have to work harder and practice more. Sometimes they need to work exceptionally long and hard to build new neuropathways to long-term memory.

*Why can information learned
on Friday be forgotten by Monday?*

Information that is of interest to the learner can be held in the hip-pocampus for short-term memory for up to 24 hours. If it is not practiced, discussed, or rehearsed, it rapidly drops away. When students cram for an exam they are filling short-term memory with the information. If it is not practiced enough, it can be retrieved for about a day, but then fades away. Several days later it is almost as if the learner had never known or knows very little of the information.

What does it really mean to be learning disabled?

Children who are selected to receive special education services due to a learning disability do not learn as quickly or easily as their nondisabled peers. Educators have picked up on successful practices for the children through observing and testing. But neuroscience helps us understand learning disabilities with more detail. In addition to the difficulty of pro-cessing speed and penetrating and releasing the learning proteins, which can cause learning disabilities, neuroscience helps us understand reading problems, as well. There are structures of the brain that need to be acti-vated for children to hear the sounds of language, the phonemes, as a necessary precursor to reading decoding. Some children do not hear the unique individual sounds and are not able to activate the specific struc-ture, the angular gyrus, to distinguish sounds. The reading decoding pathway cannot develop, and when words get too complex to memorize, the child begins to have reading problems. *Dyslexia* is a term used to define a reading disability. *Dysgraphia* is the term used for a disability that affects mathematics. Scientists have not provided as much information about children who experience problems with math, but it could be the next frontier for education to apply neuroscience.

*Does heredity or environment
have the greatest impact on intelligence?*

This is another instance of "it depends." Assuming the child has a brain that would be considered normal with all the structures in place; it is known that heredity directs the formation of the physical brain itself. The physical attributes of the human brain and how the structures work as a complex unit are studied by neurophysiology and directed by inherited DNA. *Neuroanatomy* is the study specifically of the central nervous system (the brain and the spinal cord) and the peripheral nervous system (the nerves in the cranium and the spinal cord), which connects information throughout the body. All this is inherited. *Neurology* is the study of the nervous system in respect to its structures, functions, and abnormalities. Environment affects the functions of the brain. Even in the last trimester before birth, children begin receiving signals from outside the womb. A very young child receives stimulation from the surroundings, vision, sound, touch, taste, and smell. The brain responds by making connections and constructing meaning out of what is experienced. The brain as a learning organ is built from the richness of the input the child receives from the five senses. Without that input the brain would have nothing to think about.

Neurotransmitters—Chemicals are spewed from neuron axons into the tiny gap called a synapse. Some of the chemicals fit into uptake receptors on dendrites from surrounding neurons. The chemicals create an imbalance in the receiving neurons. They in turn react with an electric jolt and spew more chemicals that race down the axon to be released into the synaptic gap.

Pathways for Reading (4)—Neuroscience has provided information about structures and their function. These structures are connected with two different pathways that develop as children learn to read. The first one that is forged is the *dorsal pathway*. Children who are beginning readers work to decode words from a pathway that is co-opted from the oral language pathway. It contains structures for recognizing sounds, identifying sounds and letters, and checking to see if words make sense. It is precise, systematic, and relatively slow at the beginning stages of reading through direct instruction. Simultaneously, as children become competent at decoding, another pathway is developed. When learners become accomplished readers they use the highly efficient and automatic *ventral route*. Many words are already known and do not have to be identified laboriously through the decoding process. A spontaneous pathway that allows the reader to read with fluency and understanding is now fused into the brain. This pathway does not stop at structures that are needed for decoding, unless a new word in introduced.

Practice for Procedures and Concepts (2)—Students often need more practice than they or their teachers plan. The hippocampus is a structure in the inner part of the brain that holds new information that can be practiced for up to 24 hours. That material, when associated with something that is already known, can be learned easier than material that is totally new. Practice that occurs over several study periods and several days eventually leaves the working memory area, the hippocampus. It is stored in other parts of the brain for long-term recall, such as the visual association area in the occipital lobes or the auditory association area of the temporal lobes. It may also be available in the frontal lobes for comprehension, analysis, or evaluation. When the information is needed again, the brain quickly and efficiently collects the information and through its extensive system of neuron networks deposits it once again in working memory for recall and use.

Sensory Memory (4)—The brain receives information from the environment continually from the five senses. It is at the point where the information is received by the thalamus that an unconscious decision is made. The information can be dropped by inhibitory neurons as if it were never received. Or it can be passed on to an association area for interpretation. If interest is strong enough, the learner can consciously think about it and hold it in working memory. (See Figure 9.9.)

Figure 9.9 Input from the senses lasts only a second or two, and it is either dropped from the system or sent to working memory for further thought.

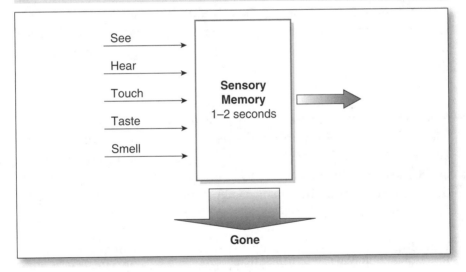

Social Emotional Learning (1, 3)—The human brain has a central area called the *limbic system*, or primitive brain. In that critical area the structures for receiving all the information from the environment, working memory, unconscious control of all the body functions, and the emotional center are located. The amygdala is a primary emotional center for initial dangers or alarming situations. This very small structure, if alarmed, has the ability to override the rest of the capabilities of the human brain. It literally can shut down the ability to focus, concentrate, and learn and to activate areas of the brain that ready the human body to fight or run from a place where danger is inherent. Knowing this, teachers are able to understand the need for a safe learning environment. They also are sensitive to students who express situations that make them uncomfortable, frightened, or even over stimulated.

Soft Systems Change (2, 8)—The human brain is limited in its capacity to learn new information or skills. Things in working memory that have been attended to are remembered for 24 hours. Items that have been practiced over an extended period of time are dropped into long-term memory and can be accessed at will. Soft systems change allows learners to master skills being emphasized before piling on a new set of requirements that require more advanced implementation. The number of tasks teachers or other adult learners are comfortably attempting to master varies with the individual. This strategy for deep learning and teaching competency for adult educators matches the efforts of the Common Core State Standards. They require a coherent movement of skills from simple to complex and complex to advanced for literacy, mathematics, and the sciences. The common core aims for students to develop deeper learning competencies.

Synapse—Tiny spaces exist between neurons' axons and dendrites to allow chemicals, neurotransmitters, to stir up activity during thinking activities. Areas of the brain stimulated by conscious or unconscious effort by the learner are involved. The chemicals set an imbalance in the neurons that have receptors for the chemicals. A chain reaction occurs as ensuing neurons become unstable electrically and involved with the message.

Working Memory (4)—Humans use short-term and long-term memory systems. Short-term memory, called *working memory*, is where the initial action takes place. Neuroscientists have identified the hippocampus in the limbic system as the place working memory appears to originate. If the idea, information, fact, or concept is practiced and associated with previous knowledge with vigor, it most likely will be transferred to other areas of the brain for long-term storage.

Figure 9.10 Information in working memory located in the hippocampus may stay for 10 to 30 seconds if it is not reinforced with concentrated effort. With practice, rehearsal, and association activities, the information can stay for about 24 hours.

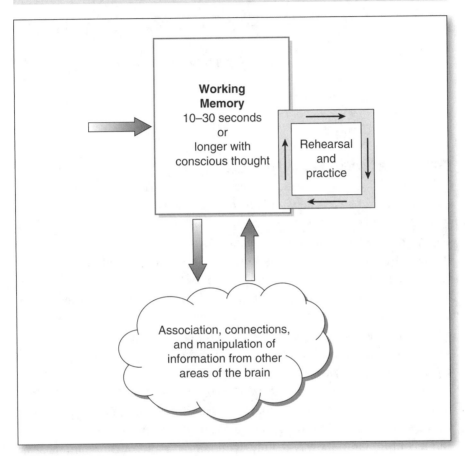

A FINAL THOUGHT

The completion of this book is only the beginning of the adventure. Everyone wins when students are prepared as learners, thinkers, and consumers of the world's challenges as it continues to advance.

References and Further Reading

The list of references and resources is noticeably different from previous publications. The age of instant information is upon us. Whereas previous references came mainly from published books and monthly journals, current research can be accessed from the Internet. As an author this becomes extremely valuable, granting almost instantaneous supportive documentation. Although there are references to published books, those are in the minority. Resources used for this book are often found on the Internet through Google searches and educational newsletters. They are timely, current, and reflective of what is happening now at schools and with teachers. However, any references to neuroscience and the workings of the learning brain are substantiated by the standards and rigor of traditional publications.

To write a book of this nature, it is extremely valuable to have a base of information about how teachers feel and think. Due to the exponential growth of the social networks available through the Internet a pulse of the teaching population is readily available. It is the author's interpretation that this is an indication of how the future will be. Books, like this one, contain bounteous resources and are indeed a precious collection for the reader. References for future reading are listed first. At the end educator resources have been accumulated.

American Educator. (2013). Concerns amid support for common core. *American Federation of Teachers, 37*(2), 3.

California State Board of Education. (2004). *Science framework for California public schools: Kindergarten through grade twelve.* Sacramento, CA: Department of Education.

California State Board of Education. (2005). *Mathematics framework for California public schools: Kindergarten through grade twelve.* Sacramento, CA: Department of Education.

California State Board of Education. (2007). *Reading/language arts framework for California public schools: Writing, speaking, reading, listening. Kindergarten through grade twelve.* Sacramento, CA: Department of Education.

Carnoy, M., & Rothstein, R. (2013). *What do international tests really show about student performance?* Washington, DC: Economic Policy Institute. Retrieved from http://www.epi.org/publication/us-student-performance-testing/

Chaffee, J. (2009). *Thinking critically* (9th ed.). New York, NY: Houghton Mifflin.

Claxton, C. S., & Murell, P. H. (1987). *Learning styles: Implications for improving educational practices.* Washington, DC: ERIC Clearing House for higher Education.

Corrin, W. (2013). *Improving college readiness in the age of the common core. MDRC.* Retrieved from http://www.mdrc.org/sites/default/files/College_readiness_030613%20%282%29.pdf

Dador, D., & Bommelje, B. (2010). *Nation's employers commit to building a stronger U.S. Workforce.* Arlington, VA: Aerospace Industries Association. Retrieved from http://www.aia-aerospace.org/newsroom/aia_news/2010/nations_employers_commit_to_building_a_stronger_u.s._workforce/

Daly, A. J. (2010). *Social network theory and educational change.* Cambridge, MA: Harvard Educational Press.

Dayal, G. (2013). Why 'neuroskeptics' see an epidemic of brain baloney. *Brain in the News, 20*(4), 4–5.

Desimone, L. M. (2011, Summer). A primer on effective professional development. *Kappan Magazine, Must Reads from Kappan, 1,* 28–31. Retrieved from http://www.gcisd-k12.org/cms/lib/TX01000829/Centricity/Domain/78/A_Primer_on_Effective_Professional_Development.pdf

Ferlazzo, L. (2013, May 5). Ways to develop creative thinking in the common core. [Web log post]. Retrieved from http://blogs.edweek.org/teachers/classroom_qa_with_larry_ferlazzo/2013/05/response_ways_to_develop_creative_thinking_in_the_common_core.html?qs=Critical+thinking+and+common+core+standards

Finn, C. E., & Porter-Magee, K. (2013). *Disappointing science standards.* Retrieved from http://www.edexcellence.net/publications/final-evaluation-of-NGSS.html

Gabriel, J. G. (2005). *How to thrive as a teacher leader.* Alexandria, VA: Association for Supervision and Curriculum Development.

Gearson, C. J. (2012, September 17). High school students need to think, not memorize. *US News Education.* Retrieved from http://www.usnews.com/education/high-schools/articles/2012/09/17/high-school-students-need-to-think-not-memorize

Gewertz, C. (2013, June 4). Into the common core: One classroom's journey. Common Core: A steep climb, Part 2 of 4. *Education Week.* Retrieved from http://www.edweek.org/ew/articles/2013/06/05/33common_ep.h32.html?tkn=VQQFjZ6yiCes%2FprKHRwrIuoKSH7ip02ozlZ6&cmp=ENL-EU-NEWS1

Gross, P. (with Buttrey, D., Goodenough, U., Koertge, N., Lerner, L. S., Schwartz, M., & Schwartz, R.). (2013). *Final evaluation of the next generation science standards.* Washington, DC: Thomas Fordham Institute. Retrieved from http://www.edexcellence.net/publications/final-evaluation-of-NGSS.html

Herman, J., & Linn, R. (2013). *The Status of Smarter Balanced and PARCC Assessment Consortia*. Retrieved from http://www.hewlett.org/library/grantee-publication/road-assessing-deeper-learning

Hewlett Foundation. (2013). *Developing transferable knowledge and skills in the 21st century*. Retrieved from http://www.hewlett.org/library/grantee-publication/education-life-and-work

Hyerle, D., Alper, L., & Curtis, S. (2004). *Student successes with thinking maps, school-based research, results, and models for achievement using visual tools.* Thousand Oaks, CA: Corwin.

Institute of Educational Sciences. (2012). *Progress in International Reading Literacy Study*. Retrieved from http://nces.ed.gov/surveys/pirls/pirls2011.asp

Kirst, M., & Venizea, A. (2010, March 10). *Improving college readiness and success for all students: A joint responsibility between K–12 and postsecondary education. Archived Information from the Secretary of Education's Commission on the future of higher Education.* Retrieved from http://www.education.com/reference/article/improve-college-readiness-success-all/

Leithwood, K., Louis, K. S., Anderson, S., & Wahlstrom, K. (2004). *How leadership influences student learning.* Retrieved from http://www.wallacefoundation.org/knowledge-center/school-leadership/key-research/Documents/How-Leadership-Influences-Student-Learning.pdf

Levine, A. (2008). Unmasking memory genes: Molecules that expose our genes may also revive our recollections and our ability to learn. *Scientific American Mind, 19*(3), 48–51.

Lieberman, A., & Mace, D. P. (2013). *Making practice public: Teacher learning in the 21st century.* Retrieved from http://www.ccte.org/wp-content/pdfs-conferences/ccte-conf-2013-spring-Final-version-JTE.pdf

Lynch, D. (2013). Academic discourse and PBL. *Edutopia.* Retrieved from http://www.edutopia.org/blog/sammamish-6-academic-discourse-PBL-danielle-lynch

Marzano, R. J., & Toth, M. D. (2013). *Teacher evaluation that makes a difference.* Alexandria, VA: Association for Supervision and Curriculum Development.

McNeil, M. (2013). Personalized learning varies for race to top districts. *Education Week.* Retrieved from http://www.edweek.org/ew/articles/2013/03/27/26rtt.h32.html?qs=Personalized+Learning+Varies

McTighe, J., & Wiggins, G. (2013). *Essential questions, opening doors to student understanding.* Alexandria, VA: ASCD.

Moroder, K. (2013). *Authentic, personalized learning: Pre- and post-technology (a case study).* Retrieved from http://blog.mcrel.org/2013/07/authentic-personalized-learning-pre-and-post-technology-a-case-study.html

National Association of Educational Progress. (2012). *The Nation's Report Card, Vocabulary results from the 2009 and 2011 NAEP Reading Assessments.* Washington, DC: National Printing Office. Retrieved from http://nces.ed.gov/nationsreportcard/pdf/main2011/2013452.pdf

Nevills, P. (2011). *Build the brain for reading, grades 4–12.* Thousand Oaks, CA: Corwin.

Nevills, P., & Wolfe, P. (2009). *Building the reading brain, pre-K–3* (2nd ed.). Thousand Oaks, CA: Corwin.

Orlich, D. C., Harder, R. J., Callahan, R. C., Trevisan, M. S., & Brown, A. H. (2007). *Teaching strategies: A guide to effective instruction.* Boston, MA: Houghton Mifflin.

Pappano, L. (2011). Differentiated instruction reexamined: Teachers weigh the value of multiple lessons. *Harvard Education Letter, 27*(3). Retrieved from http://hepg.org/hel/article/499#home

Peterson, P. E. (2011). Eighth grade students learn more through direct instruction. *Education Next.* Retrieved from http://educationnext.org/eighth-grade-students-learn-more-through-direct-instruction/

Petrilli, M. J. (2013). *Why don't schools embrace good ideas?* Washington, DC: Thomas B. Fordham Institute. Retrieved from http://www.edexcellence.net/commentary/education-gadfly-daily/flypaper/2013/why-dont-schools-embrace-good-ideas.html

Pierce, D. (2013). *How to prepare for common core testing—and why current teacher evaluation systems won't help.* Bethesda, MD: Measured Practices, Common Core. Retrieved from http://www.eschoolnews.com/2013/02/28/how-to-prepare-for-common-core-testing-and-why-current-teacher-evaluation-systems-wont-help/?ast=102&astc=9525

Pierce, D. (2013). *Tips for making the move to online assessments.* Bethesda, MD: Measured Practices, Common Core. Retrieved from http://www.eschool-news.com/2013/02/28/how-to-prepare-for-common-core-testing-and-why-current-teacher-evaluation-systems-wont-help/?ast=102&astc=9525

Poldrack, R. A., & Rodriquez, P. (2004). How do memory systems interact: Evidence from human classification and learning. *Neurobiology of Learning and Memory, 82,* 324–332.

Posani, M. (2013). Brain connectivity networks form in fetus brains, study shows. *Brain in the News, 20*(3), 1–2.

Progress in International Reading Literacy Study. (2012). *PIRLS 2001 Results.* Retrieved from http://nces.ed.gov/surveys/pirls/pirls2011.asp

Reeves, D. B. (2006). *The learning leader: How to focus school improvement for better results.* Alexandria, VA: Association for Supervision and Curriculum Development.

Robelen, E. W. (2013). Common science standards make formal debut. *Education Week.* Retrieved from http://www.edweek.org/ew/articles/2013/04/09/28science_ep.h32.html

Rothman, R. (2012). Nine ways the common core will change classroom practice. *Harvard Education Letter, 28*(4). Retrieved from http://hepg.org/hel/article/543

Schauer. K. (2013). *Message from Karen Schauer, Ed.D, GJUESD Superintendent.* Retrieved from http://www.galt.k12.ca.us/Departments/super/super.html

Schmoker, M. (2001). The "Crayola curriculum". *Education Week.* Retrieved from http://mikeschmoker.com/crayola-curriculum.html

Schmoker, M. (2003). Planning for failure? Or for school success? *Education Week.* Retrieved from http://mikeschmoker.com/planning-for-failure.html

Schmoker, M. (2010). When pedagogic fads trump priorities. *Education Week.* Retrieved from http://mikeschmoker.com/pedagogic-fads.html

Schmoker. M., & Graff, G. (2011). *More argument, fewer standards.* Retrieved from http://mikeschmoker.com/more-argument.html

Stainburn, S (2011). How can we reform science education? *Hechinger Report.* Retrieved from http://hechingerreport.org/content/how-can-we-reform-science-education_4587/

Taylor. E. (2013). *CCSD [Charleston County School District] awarded highly competitive federal grant.* Retrieved from http://www.ccsdschools.com/StrategyPlanningPartnerships/StrategyCommunications/PressReleases/documents/CCSDAwardedRTTGrant.pdf

U.S. Department of Education. (2013). *Race to the Top District—District Awards.* Retrieved from http://www2.ed.gov/programs/racetothetop-district/awards.html

Vega, V., & Terada, Y. (2013). Social and emotional techniques that help students focus on academic progress. *Edutopia.* Retrieved from http://www.edutopia.org/stw-sel-classroom-management

Wallace Foundation. (2013). *Video: Great school leadership in action.* Retrieved from http://www.wallacefoundation.org/view-latest-news/events-and-presentations/Pages/VIDEO-Great-School-Leaders-in-Action.aspx

Willingham, D. T. (2009). What will improve a student's memory? *American Educator, 32*(4), 17–25.

Wolf, M. (2007). *Proust and the squid.* New York, NY: HarperCollins.

Wolf, M., Bowers, P., & Biddle, K. (2000). RAVE-O: A comprehensive fluency-based reading intervention program. *Journal of Learning Disabilities, 33*(4). Retrieved from http://ldx.sagepub.com/search/results?fulltext=Rave-O&submit=yes&journal_set=spldx&src=selected&andorexactfulltext=and&x=8&y=12

Wolfe, P. (2010). *Brain matters: Translating research into classroom practice* (2nd ed.). Alexandria, VA: Association for Supervision and Curriculum Development.

Wolk, R. A. (2012). Common core vs. common sense. *Education Week, 32*(13), 35–40. Retrieved from http://www.edweek.org/ew/articles/2012/12/05/13wolk_ep.h32.html?tkn=SNRFRGtjYM7m81yy%2Fabgp8KwGOSGX4J7dvca&cmp=ENL-EU-VIEWS1

EDUCATOR RESOURCES—WEBSITE ADDRESSES ONLY

Clayton Christenson Institute for Disruptive Innovation, http://www.christensen-institute.org/our-mission/

Common Core State Standards for Literacy, http://www.corestandards.org/ELA-Literacy

Common Core State Standards for Mathematics. http://www.corestandards.org/Math

Common Core State Standards, Introduction, Mission http://www.corestandards.org/

Dan Meyer, educator, speaker, http://www.ted.com/speakers/dan_meyer.html

Economic Policy Institute, http://www.epi.org/issues/student-achievement/

Edutopia, online journal, http://www.edutopia.org/

Engaging Educators, https://twitter.com/engaginged

Guilford County Schools, http://www.news-record.com/news/local_news/article_f0d5a2a6-8445-11e3-a7fb-001a4bcf6878.html

Harvard Education Letter, http://hepg.org/page/hel-about

Khan Academy, http://www.khanacademy.org/about

Lindsay Unified School District, http://www.lindsay.k12.ca.us/District/Department/689-Performance-based-System

Owl and Mouse Software, http://www.yourchildlearns.com/alpsci.htm

Sammamish High School, home page, http://www.bsd405.org/sammamish/

Share my Lessons, by teachers for teachers, http://www.sharemylesson.com/high-school-teaching-resources/

TED, Technology, Entertainment, Design, http://www.ted.com/pages/about

The Curriculum Corner, http://www.thecurriculumcorner.com/

The Next Generation Standards for Science for States by States, http://www.nextgenscience.org/next-generation-science-standards

U.S. Government (2013). Race to the Top Grant, http://www2.ed.gov/programs/racetothetop/index.html

Index

Note: In page references, f indicates figures and t indicates tables.

CORWIN
A SAGE Company

The Corwin logo—a raven striding across an open book—represents the union of courage and learning. Corwin is committed to improving education for all learners by publishing books and other professional development resources for those serving the field of PreK–12 education. By providing practical, hands-on materials, Corwin continues to carry out the promise of its motto: **"Helping Educators Do Their Work Better."**